Are You Ready?

VOLUME IV

Conversation with Angels

Are You Ready?

Dror B. Ashuah

Epigraph Books
Rhinebeck, New York

ISBN 978-1-948796-92-7

Library of Congress Control Number: 2019914862

Book design by Colin Rolfe
Cover photo by D.B. Ashuah

To continue the conversation: www.conversationwithangels.com

Epigraph Books
22 East Market Street, Suite 304
Rhinebeck, New York 12572
(845) 876-4861
epigraphps.com

"You have slept millions and millions of years.
Why not wake up this morning?"
Kabir

Dedicated to My father, Igal Ashuah,
who passed away on 2/26/18.
I love you.

Contents

Are You Ready? Messages

Preface

Publishing a book is like giving birth. You never know what is hiding in the womb until the "delivery." Once born, you may nourish, love, and support it, but eventually, your "creation" ends up following its own path, completely separate from the one who birthed it.

So why should you read "Are You Ready?" If you came across this book, it is no coincidence. It may signal that indeed you are ready to grow, expand, and move away from your current predicament. Your expanded self may have invited this book to support you by illuminating your path and holding you in a place of love.

After you have read it, consider leaving it in a public space where someone else might discover it. This book was meant for those who came in this lifetime to be the lighthouses, and to offer you support through the challenges you will invariably face in the process. The role of lighthouses is to help show others safe passage on their journey. If you are one, then I invite you to read any of the four volumes: "Conversation With Angels"; "And So Be It"; "It's Time"; and "Are You Ready?" Know that you are deeply loved and that you are not alone.

Every word in this book has been charged with love. The energy emanating from these transmissions is subtle, but the vibration will permeate your cells and begin to activate your inner light, nudging it to vibrate higher, expanding your field of consciousness. The good news is that whether you can feel these effects or not doesn't even matter, regardless it works.

All that is asked of you is to read "Are You Ready?" with an open heart and mind. Scan the book at your own pace and allow yourself the gift of its love. As a result, your natural capacity to feel love will grow while deepening your sense of self-love. You will expand your understanding of your power and increase your ability to manifest more love in your life and align with what serves your growth best. You will begin to imbibe the idea that everything in your life begins and ends with the choices you make. You will come to understand that you are the master of your own life; once realized, you may start to take full responsibility for yourself and what happens around you. You will begin to use discernment, inviting what serves, and discarding what doesn't help you.

"Are You Ready?" is not meant to be studied, nor do you need to memorize the words or concepts found within these pages. You are encouraged to be in a receptive, open, calm, and supportive space while reading it.

Please be aware that opening and expanding in such a way can have effects that are not always perceived as positive or joyful. What challenges could possibly accompany such gifts? Whenever you grow, you can no longer go back to the person you once were. A potential consequence is that you may lose certain friends or even close family members that are not aligned with your new path. You may find existing relationships are fundamentally challenged. At the very least, primary connections will be forced to grow. Since you cannot "un-know" what you now know, tension is created, which may lead to "growing pains," which I personally experienced along my path.

As a result of reading this book, your choices regarding work may change; your taste buds and clothing style, and even your skin may change. You very may well slowly but noticeably become a different person than the one you were before. Like a caterpillar that goes through a cocoon phase before becoming a butterfly, this growing process is not reversible; once transformed, you cannot go back, nor would you probably want to.

The fate of humanity is in the hands of those who lead the way, shining their light for others. If more of us make choices based on a unity consciousness that emanates from the heart, radiating a vibration of love, then together, we can create a field that changes the current paradigm.

At the same time, you may be challenged because your environment doesn't want you to change. The light-path is not for the meek. It is meant for warriors. You must be willing to die and be reborn to a new, unfamiliar reality, one that is potentially quite different from that of your beloved, your parents, culture, or religion. Do know that this is the path, and a natural part of the process of transformation.

A little about me:

I had a somewhat unique upbringing growing up the second child of six siblings, four brothers, and two sisters on the Israeli Northern border. We lived on a Kibbutz, which is an idealistic communal lifestyle that had been common in Israel during the time I was being raised. I grew up in a secular environment in which angels were never discussed. I am secular to this day. After finishing high school, I completed my requisite time in the Israeli army serving in an Elite Special Forces unit. In my mid-twenties, I attended The Massachusetts College of Art and Design in Boston, where I received my B.A. Later, I attended Harvard University, where I earned a Master's degree in Psychology and Human Development. Coming to the United States without a penny to my name, I managed to create and run a successful business, which I subsequently sold, and decided to retire just before my 42nd birthday to be a full-time stay-at-home Dad.

Until 2007, my life was, by Western standards, successful and fulfilling. I was married to an artist, with whom I had a beautiful child that I adored, and we occasionally traveled to exotic places. I had ample time on my hands.

December 10th, 2007 would forever change my trajectory. On a rainy day at Starbucks, an unlikely meeting with a self-proclaimed angel would transform me in ways I would never have imagined possible. (Interestingly enough, I first arrived in the United States on December 10th, 1987, exactly twenty years prior to my angelic encounter.)

While I faced a headwind from some of the people nearest and dearest to me, at the same time, I received immense support and counsel from my closest friends.

Being guided in such a direct way enabled an entirely new world and dimension to become accessible to me. I felt an enormous, ecstatic love for humanity and a luminous potential future around the corner if we collectively connected to our hearts.

In all of my books, the message that keeps repeating over and over is that YOU are the ultimate authority of your life, and no one in the world knows better than you concerning your path.

You may ask, so where did these messages come from? Who are those alleged angels and who is the person you met at Starbucks twelve years ago? The Hebrew word for angel is "Maalaach," meaning a messenger of light. The information contained in this book draws from a collective of "guides" also known as angelic beings.

Some of us are on a path to become messengers, healers, and lighthouses, a path chosen before we descended into the birth canal. Our journey is to wake up in this lifetime as to why we are here and to fulfill our purpose by creating bridges of light to a higher vibration, to a more evolved unity-conscious-based community, to a new paradigm.

I volunteered to be one of the people who facilitate in making this information available at this particular time. This "access" is open to all of us throughout life. I chose to listen and take down these notes.

It has been eleven years since the first book, "Conversation with Angels," came out.

I wish to make one point clear; I do not possess special powers. I have no channels open to Angels that anyone else doesn't also possess. I am like you.

I conclude with this declaration because it is my observation over the years that, time and time again—after working with hundreds, maybe thousands of individuals—people will give away their power to those they believe to possess even greater power. I would also like to avoid any projections that I somehow hold unique abilities. My power and choices are equal in the playing field of life to anyone else. The tools I use are available to everyone.

I choose a clean lifestyle so that I can stay attuned to these subtle energies and hear my guides' whispers. I know that these messages are available directly from the source to anyone who chooses to listen. I encourage you to try.

This book, "Are You Ready?" is the fourth and final book in the "Conversation with Angels" series. It concludes the series with all of the unfiltered messages that I have received to date since December 10th, 2007. It should be read the same way as my other books. Think of a question, or ask to be guided, and randomly open the book. Whatever page you land on, that's your message. You may find it to be very accurate. I do not recommend reading it like a novel. It's best to read one message a day, and always with the same intention.

Please know that the voices in these books communicate directly to you. The texts speak of our existence in a circle where nothing is linear; therefore, all potentials are present.

If there is any one message to take away from all these pages, it is for you to know that you are unconditionally loved. Your choices are all honored, not judged, and your primary mission is to learn how to fully embrace and love yourself. When you are in a place of self-love, you ripple that love to everyone and everything around you, illuminating their path. And so be it.

With immense gratitude,
Dror

December 10th, 2007

It was the first time I had left my peaceful apartment the whole day. As I stepped outside, I was carried away by a crowd with umbrellas and large coats, a stream of people negotiating left and right to make their way and still not collide with anyone. It smelled fresh from the light rain that had just begun.

I was walking on Broadway and behind me was a French couple pointing to the tip of the City Hall building. I always wondered, with all the beautiful buildings in Europe, what would impress Europeans visiting New York City. Christmas was around the corner and I could feel the energy of excitement and holiday shopping buzz all around me. Then I noticed the scaffolding on the corner of Broadway and Reade Street where the Starbucks coffee shop was. There was a black man dressed in all white with thick black curly hair. He was hiding from the rain under the canopy of the scaffolding. There was something about him that seemed unreal or out of context. His shoes were white and he had the kind of loose dress that one associates with the holy man of India. He noticed my stare and smiled at me with his eyes. I passed by him and entered the coffee shop. There were only a few people inside. I bought my treat and went to my usual place at the far back of the café to enjoy my moment. As I took off my coat, I saw the man in white standing right behind me very close, almost too close for New York standards. Behind him were two more men, also wearing white. I looked around and no one seemed to notice what was going on. I thought to myself, something does not add up here. I looked back again, verifying that I was not daydreaming and they were still there. This is New York and anything can happen here, I said to myself. I sat down and the black man in white pulled up a chair on the other side of the table and said in the softest voice, "We wish to speak with you, is that all right?"

My heart started to pump a bit faster. I thought maybe they wanted money but I said OK anyway, and then all of a sudden, I felt the noise around me quiet down. As if time stopped for a moment, and I could no longer hear the holiday music playing above me, nor the Spanish-speaking couple two tables down. The man said, "We want to speak to you about you and we wish you to take notes." Normally I would have said, "... and *who* are you?" However, looking at him, I felt as if I had to do what he said, as he emitted an energy that made me feel like melted butter. I pulled out my notebook and pen, and without saying anything I waited. (I always carry my notebook and pen in case some brilliant idea will cross my path. It is a habit from way back.) Somehow I felt that there was something so unusual about this that I had to just follow and flow with it. The man started to speak in a slow, soft tone. He had a low baritone voice. As he spoke, I felt so much love coming from him. The other two were right beside him sitting as well. I remember thinking that I did not see additional chairs at my table, and that it was strange. He spoke as a group and this is what he said: "We are angels like you and it is time we met. Please take notes." So I did.

New York
The Buffet

It is our intention to love you. *Why?* you may ask. Because through the energy of love we communicate and connect to you; we are all linked through the invisible strings of love. *Why then is there not more of this love energy on this planet? Why is there so much anger and hate?* you may wonder. It is because you must choose. The choice is always yours at any given moment. Although we give you love, it does not necessarily mean that you choose to accept it. The fact remains that we love you regardless of your choice. Whether you choose to use our love or ignore it, you are loved just the same.

Doesn't this fact tell you something about spirit? Your learning is sacred. Your choices are sacred.

Where are we headed? you may ask. You are headed to where you choose to be. If we had to predict, we would say that you are headed to a higher place than ever before. We feel that your choices are such that you ascend continuously. *Why can't we feel it?* you may ask. It is again your choice whether to feel it or not. You have a big table full of different kinds of food: from nutritious to junk, from divine taste to sour and spoiled. Some of you are used to sour and spoiled and may choose to eat it out of habit, some will choose to try the nutritious, and some will not touch the "good food" because they do not trust it. The food is available to you. The buffet-style table is filled with an abundance of choices. The higher you vibrate, the more selection you will find. *How do you know what food is good and what will give you a bellyache*? you may ask. Your intent will lead you through your feeling centers. Spoiled food gives a foul smell; similarly, a bad choice emits a foul smell. Fresh, nutritious food offers a healthy, fresh, delicious smell. Your feeling center can be activated the same way as your sense of smell. As you choose to smell the food before you bite into it, you may choose to check in with your feeling center and sense how your choice smells. If it smells spoiled and you sense you will become sick after you eat it, why would you choose it?

We wish to explain that for each choice you make there is a color, a scent, a vibration, and energy. Just as a painter creates a picture based on the colors and brush strokes he chooses, so do you create the picture of your reality based on the ingredients you choose to mix. It is, however, a multidimensional picture and not a two-dimensional picture. The picture you may think you create in 2D looks very different when you go beyond 4D. Therefore, things are not always what they seem. More often than not it is quite the contrary. It is again the choice of the human to use the feeling center and go beyond the surface. Your emotions and your feelings are your biggest gifts, if you trust them and use them.

We have observed humanity for a long time. There was a time when your feeling centers were connected to the planet and you just "knew" what choice created what reactions. You have, over millennia, moved away from your emotions and feelings, discarding them as feminine or irrational. You have moved away from the divine, feminine side of yourselves to the rational, masculine side. By doing so, you have created imbalance within yourselves and your relationships to the planet. It is now, from our perspective, time for the pendulum to swing back. Some of you will choose to use the new tools available at this time to make new choices. These "new tools" will work better than ever because they are in line with the direction the pendulum is swinging. Those who will choose to disregard the new tools and make choices based on the old "rational tools" will find that the logic they were using is no longer working in the same linear fashion. In fact, many will find that 2+2 will equal 5. In such an environment, many of the assumptions that some of you will make will be proven wrong, and the results will be disappointing. Those, however, who choose to open up to how things feel rather than adding up the numbers, will find many doors open and more power to express, manifest, and stay balanced. You are experiencing a shift of paradigm. This shift manifests on all levels of consciousness and therefore it is expressed through your biology as well. You are becoming more enabled than ever as a human. It is a wonderful time to smell the flowers, to slow down and "feel" your selves.

It is a time for celebration of your new potential, your new you's. *How would we celebrate?* you may ask. We know who you are. Some of you have fears, doubts, anxiety, sickness, and everything seems to be going haywire. We are here to give you a hug and tell you that what you see is not what we see. We see you growing and learning to walk like a child who learns to use her legs to find balance. Of course, at times she falls and hurts her knees, maybe even bleeds a little. But this child we are seeing is determined to walk—and to walk by herself. We see a beautiful child on target to walk on her own soon. You may ask us, *how do you see that?* We see it because we can see your potential. The sums of your choices are heading toward that potential. Humanity is walking as if it has a compass and knows where North is. Learn to check within. Do not consult the newspapers, TV, or any other media for that matter. They will all tell you that things are gloomy. There is still a strong residue of fear-based economics, trades, and actions. Those modes, however, are weakening daily. Nevertheless, there are those who are still fighting to maintain their strong hold on your reality. They delay your shift in consciousness through fear. Fear blocks progress. Control blocks progress and creates fear. Understand that you are powerful—more powerful than you ever have been. You have the tools, and all you need to do is to choose. Every time you choose light over darkness you have tipped the balance and brought the shift that much closer. You do not need to be in politics or run for president to change this balance. You are who you are and who you are is just as loved as the next one. Each one makes a difference, and every new light that is ignited shows the way for many who are in the dark. The power of the one is immense. It is again inter-dimensional, where 1+1=100,000. This is how powerful each and every one of you is who makes a choice every single day. And so be it.

Foreword from the Angels

We love you so and this is just the beginning. We come to you in this form because you have asked us to bring this information to you. Some of you may ask, *but where is it coming from, really*?

Our simple answer is that this information is coming from the circle. Some of you may ask if this is what some call channeling. With all love we wish to tell you that many of you misunderstand the idea behind channeling. You are all channeling all the time. It is your linear perception that keeps you from the awareness that you are many things and in many places simultaneously.

Channeling from where we sit, is becoming clear enough to realize the source of the information you are receiving. Like your modern-day radio, if you tune into a FM station that transmits classical music, you will say now I am tuned to that station. Now, when you change the station to classic rock, you will know that indeed you have changed the station. The channeler knows which station she is receiving the message from and can tune to it at will. With all love we wish to tell you that in your day to day life, many of you are exposed to so much noise that you are not walking in the awareness of the circle. It requires you to be in a subtle place to know which music comes from which station.

You are a vessel and that is your mission. It is you who must allow the energy of divinity through so you can become the unlimited multidimensional being that you are. Indeed there are some who channel a particular being from the other side bringing forth specific information. This is not the source of this information. We are angels and we are part of you. You are a group and we are part of your group. You may say to us *yes, but you said that you come from here and there and you do this and that.* Yes, we do and so do you.

You are much larger than you can ever imagine and your group is busy in creating things that you cannot even grasp. This information is coming from a source that is in you. *What if we do not get this information and it does not resonate?* some of you may wonder. With a hug we wish to impart to you that if this information does not resonate with you, know that there is never a judgment, but it is not coming from you and therefore it is not for you. We ask you then to celebrate your diversity and the grandness of your circle and keep searching for your mission. It is never a one size fits all. You all have missions but they are all suited perfectly for each one of you. The ones who were meant to read these messages will know it immediately and without a doubt.

The simple explanation is that you are linear and this information comes from the circle. It connects to the circular part in you. Those of you who created this information will feel that these words resonate fully with your being. Those who will resonate are the creators and the information, although brought through one human, is meant to allow the many to shift vibration. There are many layers to each of the messages. Each message is meant to address an angel at a particular time on their journey. In essence, all of the messages combined are just like an alarm clock. They are meant to wake you up on the cellular level to what you already know and remind you that it is time to get out of bed. You have chosen us to bring this to you and not vice versa. You are the creator and when you go to the store and ask to purchase an alarm clock, the store's clerk hands you one. We are the store's clerk and we follow your request. *But who are you?* some of you may persist. We are part of you, the reader.

We wish to take you by the hand and ask you to fly with us into the magical land of the circle. There, there is no time and no space like the one you occupy on earth. All is multilayered and happens simultaneously. The messages must come through one that has achieved harmonious resonance and a high frequency so the messages can flow without much distortion. There are always limitations to the messages as they are being delivered through words, and use the vocabulary of the one who transcribes it.

With a hug we wish to tell you that the real purpose of the message is for you to wake yourself up to your own potential. Many of you may say, *I like this message and I do not like that message. This is from a channel but this is more scientific and it is from the writer's knowledge.* We ask you to not place boxes around the circle. The source is you. You can put it in the hand of the author or an entity, or you can attribute it to this being or that being but it is you and you will know it fully when you read them.

We love you and we wish to tell you that you are the author and you will know it because it will feel as if you could have written it. It will feel so familiar. We also told you with a hug that these messages are not meant for all of you. If you are not the "author" you will know it as well and there is never a judgment. It does not mean that you are not spiritual enough or divine enough. It only means that you are on a different mission and you may want to keep searching for that which resonates with your mission. You are all angels, all divine and all on missions. No mission is more honorable or prestigious than the next. You are so dearly loved and we ask you to become that which you are: a master in disguise walking with the knowledge of your own divinity.

The writer, editor, and publisher of these messages are simply your messengers as they cater to your intent, bringing you that which you have requested. Do not look at the typeface, the format, or the book cover as they are just tools. These messages act as a conveyor of the energy of love which aims to link you with you and to wake you up to your own divinity.

With a hug we wish to impart to you that Love energy acts and harmonizes with your cells facilitating healing in your body when it is appropriate. It is again not the tools which heal you but it is you who heals yourself through intent. We wish to tell you that these messages do not come from an entity or a channel; they come from you the reader. They come to those of you who have requested them. Those who have requested them will be guided to these messages and will know instantly that they are for them. Those of you who have not asked for these messages will not be able to finish a single page as it will appear alien or too confusing.

You are magnificent and we see you as geometric patterns moving about; these messages correspond to your geometry and each message links to a moment in time in the cycle you call human life. We ask you to read this book like a recipe book. When you crave a certain type of food, look through the menu and pick the one that seems the most appetizing. Use your feeling and allow the correct message to present itself. Be playful and allow that which comes from the circle to celebrate with you the shifting of you and the planet. You are changing and the planet is changing. Your vibration is increasing and the molecules around you dance differently than they used to.

It is the grandest time in your history as humans on this planet and nothing you know will stay the same. All must shift with the shifting of your planet. It is your intent that gives the push for this change and we ask you to become peaceful with all that is around you. We ask you to use love in all your interactions and relationships. We ask you to become the master that you are at every moment that you breathe. There are many who await your awakening.

There are trillions of us who support your journey and celebrate every light that shines with its own divinity. We ask you to be in the now and know that there is no other time than the time you are in and with a sweet touch we ask you to wake up to your divinity and wear the outfit of the master as it is calling you. And so be it.

Are You Ready?

Messages

A Tree

When the dust settles and the wind ceases to blow, you wake up and your landscape seems so much different than how it appeared a moment earlier. You have closed your eyes just for a moment and that was enough for a profound change. Time is no longer linear, and processes which would have taken centuries to unravel happen as if in a mere day. The quality of energy now permeating your planet is like rain that falls on a tree, and the tree gratefully stands there, present, silent, allowing nature to nourish it. This same tree does not chase the sun. It simply grows from its roots, reaching ever higher. This wise tree knows that all the conditions are ripe for it to become a powerful, mature tree and it does not need to go anywhere in search. The tree is you and the conditions for your growth are right where you are. You do not need to search for the sun, nor do you need to bring the rain. Your role is to be present and offer gratitude.

We do not see the sun nor do we feel the rain, you say. *We have been looking for the right conditions to grow and they are like a mirage, moving away each time we get closer. We continually ask for peace, we ask for harmony, we ask for abundance and to move higher, and it seems that no one is really listening. Why is that so,* you wish to know?

For each of your wishes there is a melody; for each of your requests there is a shape. Each time you ask, your request is registered in the great halls of records through a unique frequency and nothing ever gets lost. We see you ask for peace while being angry at the world for not obeying your request. After all, you wished for a beautiful, benevolent reality that will benefit all. We hear many wish for abundance while being fearful that it will not show up in time to cover their bills. We see you sing the melodies of your dreams, and as soon as these melodies are expressed and sent to the halls, you create other frequencies which negate the initial melody and what arrives to the register at the great halls is incoherent, weak communication, which looks very different from the one you believe you sent.

I wish to move forward and it feels as if I am moving backward, you say.

And we answer as always, with a deep reverence to your journey: There is no forward nor is there a backward where we come from. You always move in circles and as you grow the circle stretches into a spiral. The only real movement is within you.

Your wishes are frequencies that are the basis for all movement in your physical universe. Your wish is a set of instructions sent from source energy to its environment and this set of orders must be obeyed, as it is a free will universe you are occupying, and there is no authority above your own free will.

So why is this world in such a state of disorder, you ask?

And we reply: because of you.

What you see all around you is the manifestation of your collective thought patterns and yes, it is neither harmonious nor beautiful. Beauty is order, balance, and harmony. Your environment obeys your wishes, and as you look all around and realize in despair that what you have created is not what you intended, you may begin to realize how to finally utilize your power to return to balance. This is why we are here, to sound the bell and awaken you to your power because you have been asleep for a long time, the ship is adrift, and you are moving through treacherous waters. You are the captain of your ship, and unless you are awakened, your ship will continue to sail at the mercy of the waves and winds.

All of you have equal power to bring about the reality that serves you and to override the reality, which is in disservice to you. It is simple to begin and gets more complicated as the circle stretches and spirals upward. As you walk and act, you emit frequencies. The more harmonious these frequencies are, and the more aligned with the energy of love, the more magnificent the vision you create.

I have been meditating, sending light, and visualizing world peace, and the world is no closer to peace. What have I been doing wrong, you inquire?

If your world is not more peaceful as a result of your practice, you may want to adjust your practice.

I am not talking about my world, but the world at large, you say.

Be the tree, we say to you, and do not go on worrying about the well-being of the forest before you've mastered being the tree. Your most powerful contribution to the forest that you are part of is being the most magnificent tree.

Why is it so, you ask?

Like the tree, your mission is to absorb light and at the same time be rooted in the soil and a part of Gaia. Like an antenna, you are a conduit to frequencies of light, transforming light into energy and love. Love is the air that humanity needs to inhale for it to ascend higher.

Being the pure conduit is your role. The tree does not worry about the state of the forest because it knows that it is the forest. Once you've mastered your own practice, experiencing peace, harmony, balance, and feeling loved, you have changed the forest because you are the forest—each and every one of you.

This is not new to you but what we are about to say next may be new and may also change the way you view your life. It is not only that you are the forest and you are the tree, you are also the soil, the rain, the air, the sun, and the stars. When your reality is aligned, exhaling and inhaling love, you change the paradigm for all.

But we've heard that before, you say.

Be the tree, we answer, and be patient, we say with a smile.

Feel the energy around you and connect to the truth that is streaming to you from above and below. Love is your language, and there is a need for only one light to fully decode the language of love and create a union that is recorded in the great halls for peace on Earth to become your reality, as if overnight, and this is your potential.

You have over seven billion people occupying this place you call home, and if one sounds the pure tonal frequency it will change your tonal range altogether. This has always been the potential and some of your sacred myths called this frequency "the Messiah."

What, you may ask in bewilderment?

That angel who has the potential to bring about a shift in the tonal range of consciousness on your precious planet is not chosen in advance, and it can be any of you at any given moment.

What are the mechanics of such a process, you ask?

As the conductor of a symphony, you may choose at any given moment to use the baton in such a way that the entire orchestra will change the tune it is playing. Once the conductor makes the sign, each inhabitant on this planet will be asked, in multidimensional space, "Do you wish to accept the new melody?" When the collective gives permission for the melody's tonal range to change, your reality may dramatically shift.

This cannot be, you say. *No one can change the reality for all.*

It happened before and it will happen again.

We realize that this statement may be controversial, so we will explain it metaphorically to make it easier to comprehend. You are all connected, all of the time, through invisible strings. The fact that you do not see these strings does not negate their existence. You are all moving along a continuum of sorts, from one state of awareness to higher states by collecting different experiences and responding to these experiences, making choices lifetime after lifetime. Your groove was paved for you up until now so you would move within a charted path, sometimes slower and other times faster. Your road was known and your choices along your path determined your progress. You have reached a level on your evolutionary journey as one consciousness exploring itself, to a place where you are no longer moving on a predetermined path, and all roads and possibilities are available to you. Spiritually and physically your world becomes more connected than ever before, as if gravity pulls all of you closer. The more connected you are the faster a ripple can reach all of you from the core center of the circle.

How can one affect the whole, you ask?

It happens all the time, but we speak here of a unique frequency that must be aligned with the same trajectory taken by your ascending planet, moving from the Earth to the heart, or from first and second chakras to the fourth chakra. You represent the micro, and the planet the macro. Once the alignment between consciousness and Gaia is perfected, the baton will give the sign to shift the whole orchestra to a new melody.

What must I do to align, you ask?

The secret answer to this mystery is hidden in the melding and merging of the masculine and feminine into one field of energy represented by the sphere. This sphere must ascend from the Earth to the heart center, opening it fully to become one with all.

Why is it so hard to achieve?

There are only two ways to achieve this melody: for the angel to create a perfect masculine/feminine balance within him/herself and vibrate the oneness rippling frequency of love coming from a place of perfect balance. The other road is for two, through love, to merge their polarities to become one and create a ripple that is perfectly aligned with the highest frequency of the heart. The two must dance in such away after clearing all inner blocks and heaviness so their polarities will flow without obstructions through the heart.

Each of you who engages in moving higher must work on opening their heart as it is your "now" center replacing the "mind" that was dominating your planet for the past few thousands of years.

What is this talk of being "the Messiah?"

We use the word allegorically to describe a possibility for an immense shift that is a potential in each of you who is working to open her heart. You are a vibration and your reality is symbolic, so each act, thought, or feeling is expressed through shapes, lights, colors, melodies, and tones. Each of you represents the whole, like the code of your DNA, which contains your entire blueprint, whether it is embedded in your toenail or a strand of hair. You are a holographic blueprint of your universe, the planet, and humanity, so in each of you lies dormant the potential to change the tune for the whole. This tune is not a religious tune nor is it a tune of devotion, sacred text, hymn, or mantra. An angel who aligns her vibration, shape, light, color, tone, and melody with the highest potential of Earth's evolutionary melody activates the portal which ripples the new melody to all humanity, creating an immense shift in the entire consciousness which you are a part of.

The power of the one is immense, and the power of the two who become one through love can change your storyboard. If you are still in doubt, know that you are loved just the same. In each of you lies the seed for a majestic tree, and we ask you to know that you have all you need to play your most magnificent role at this time, on this planet, and so be it.

The Threshold

The Earth turns and turns, and you ride on her, minding your business. At times, many are oblivious to the fact that you are moving through infinite space that is vast and expansive.

Many of you walk a path guided by tunnel vision that identifies threats, problems, wishes, and wanting, rather than just being, celebrating this divine journey through space and time, embracing the mysteries of existence itself.

The celestial bodies come in due time to remind you to look up and celebrate your membership in the exclusive club of multidimensional beings, united in love with your galactic family.

To fly means to be above your day-to-day drama and see the beauty in all that encompasses existence. You were meant to fly; you were meant to soar above and to be part of the cosmos.

Why are you telling us stories? We are busy and we have lives where we have to take care of business.

If you were meant to just be here and take care of business don't you think that your world would be friendlier to this reality? Do you find that your taking care of business as usual is rewarding to you? Do you find magic in your life? Do you find miracles wherever you go? Do you feel gratitude for everything and everyone that is part of your life? Do you feel loved? Are you full or empty?

Your "real business" as you call it, is precisely that—to fly while being present in your body, connected to your breath and heartbeat.

At times you look around and see all that is taking place and you wonder, what is happening? Why am I here? Intuitively you know of your vastness, of your power, of your contracts, and of your mission. You pause at times, knowing that where you are and where your dreams are parted ways a long time ago. All that is left is a void—emptiness despite the fact that everything seems to be "okay" and "fine."

You are so much more than you were ever taught to believe. If you could only see yourself for just a moment through our eyes, you would begin to dance to your own divine melody and never stop.

There are doorways that were meant for you to walk through, and in each lifetime, you may pass by many of them and never open a single one. And then comes a cycle—and sacred this cycle is—when you become aware of the doors, and one by one you open them and walk through. Each door opened creates a pulse that changes the universal beat around you. Each door opened introduces a new frequency to your reality, and each new reality allows you to soar higher. This is your time and your mission, to open these doors and walk through. You are living in a time where many become aware of the "doors" and you face a choice, either to walk through or to turn around and pretend that you didn't see them. Many of you find yourselves walking hesitantly as if not to awaken yourselves. You fear this awakening because it is uncomfortable to acknowledge that you are not aligned with your truth, with your mission, and with the reason you came to be. Each door opened represents the dying of an aspect of the self and the rebirth of another. You know that once you open that door, you can never go back and close it, and you must pass through. Humans fear the unknown, but you come here for that same reason. You come to explore the mysteries of life, yet many wish to know what will happen to them and pray at night for security and safety.

Why am I so afraid, you wish to know?

You fear that you have something to lose. You fear that you will be lost and never find that which you are looking for. You fear that you will not be loved. All three aspects of fear are the illusion you must pierce through and shutter. You have nothing to lose, only to gain, when you let go and surrender your illusion of control. When you do not have a specific destination you can never get lost, and most importantly, you are always loved. It is your birthright to be loved despite, at times, the harsh physical reality that tells you a different story.

I am tired, what now?

Look up and watch the night sky, keep your eyes gazing at the stars, and breathe deeply. Become one with Venus, watch the moon and feel its radiance. Your galactic family is watching you and it is time you say hello.

If I had known that there is something better out there I would surely open all doors, but I don't, some silently think. *I need guarantees because I do not wish to take risks and waste my life.*

No life is ever wasted, and whichever way you choose to go is sacred and offers learning. There are some of you who came here for a special mission this lifetime. This mission is second to none. It is one that was foretold by your ancestors and one that you came here to fulfill. You knew of it when you were preparing to descend into the birth canal; you knew it when you emerged from your mother's womb; you knew it when you were growing up, and you know it now. This knowing was never lost. This is the difference between you and many others. You did not forget. You've always known that you are here on Earth for a special mission—you just did not have the instructions yet laid out in front of you. These instructions are now available and will be presented to you when you open your door.

Each of you comes here to accomplish specific learning for your own growth and add to the luminosity of the whole. Some in this constellation act as the wax, others as the wick, and others as the flame. Your role is to be the candle-holder. Without your awakening, there would be no context for the wax, wick, and flame to exist.

No mission is greater than the other, but some missions build the foundations for all others. For Earth to exist as a home for consciousness to express itself in the physical, you need certain conditions to manifest. Without breathable air and drinkable water, your physical body will not survive. Air and water molecules know of this contract and represent an aspect of consciousness that lays the foundation for physical expression to thrive. Same is with your mission.

You are here to build what was never built before. You are to build a bridge of light so that your current vibrational rate can be linked with the next higher octave to create a smooth organic transition higher. Earth's vibrational rate is ascending, and your mission is to build the bridge for human angels to move in alignment with Gaia and recalibrate their frequency, so you may continue and thrive on this journey of exploration and growth.

What if I said that I do not believe it and do not choose to partake in this mission?

We hug you and ask you to feel in your heart how loved you are for being here at this time walking blindfolded. All we are doing is gently removing the blindfold that covers your eyes, and letting you see where you are and what it is that you came here to do. If after your eye covers are removed you choose to keep your eyes closed, know that you are loved just the same and never judged. Your choices are sacred above all.

Will anything bad happen to me as a result of my choice?

It is funny to us that you are told over and over again of your power, but you are so quick to hand your power over to whomever. We are not more powerful than you are, in fact, no one is. If anything "bad" will happen to you it will be from your choice to awaken to or accelerate a journey that is not fulfilling your soul's highest path. No "harm" will come from any source other than you as a result of you not following your mission. We are placing "bad" and "harm" in quotes because there is really no such thing. It may be your perception that something serves you at one point in time and does not serve you at another (and you assign plus or minus signs), but your greater knowing experiences everything as plus. When you experience an event as painful, horrible, and harmful, you truly register it in such terms, but your soul does not. It sees all of it as just one brush stroke in a masterpiece that makes you who you are. You are eternal and vast, and whatever you choose to experience on this plane of existence is a sacred aspect of your learning and desire to explore being human, and to expand as a result.

So what now?

It's time to choose whether you follow what you know to be your truth, or you close your eyes.

What happens if I say yes and choose to walk my highest path?

If we skip the description of the party, the fireworks, the high fives, and the congratulations, all you need to really do is follow your heart and open those doors you know need to be opened. You will not need to imagine them or create them as they will appear clearly in front of you. Each time you walk through the threshold and cross to the other side a new melody will sound. This melody is your sign that a new frequency has just been introduced to all. This is the gift and the responsibility of those of you who are to hold the context and foundation for the light to illuminate.

What should I expect?

You have come here to experience magic and miracles, and to fly. This is what you may expect. All the heaviness that you hold onto for dear life will be challenged and tested, presenting you with opportunities to become more transparent, lose weight, ascend in vibration, and illuminate your planet.

Will I be happier than now?

We cannot say that you will be happier, but we can tell you that your glow will be seen from your satellites, and you will know deep inside that you are where you were meant to be.

How should I proceed?

It's your time to move out of your shell and emanate the messages that you have been receiving to those who were meant to hear them. It is not you who is emanating, but the light emanating through you, so you must be present and allow. It is not your role to create light but to allow light through. You are a vessel acting as a conduit.

Am I to do anything?

You are to do plenty, and the doing will not feel like doing but more like allowing. You are not expected to push any agenda or build lofty structures that will serve some lofty ideas. Your role is to be in your heart and live from your heart. Your role is to open to what is to come and embrace it without judging.

Do I need to know what is coming?

You need to know that your planet is in the midst of a fundamental change and you chose to take part in this sacred process. You have been shown visions, and those visions will manifest when the time is ripe. Your role is to watch and allow, move to the melody, and have no vested interest in the outcome—except for the outcome to serve all through love and grace supporting a vision for Earth and all her inhabitants to fulfill the highest potential at this time.

How do I know that I am walking the right path?

Once you open a door, you can no longer close it and you must walk through. Same here, once you have followed your highest vision it will be the vision that comes to you and it is the right path for you. You will feel it deeply and if it is not yours your light will not allow it to come near you.

What's the next step?

If we tell you the next step you will keep asking questions but will be no wiser than before. Know that you are to walk where your heart is. The instructions are stored in your heart and your role is to keep your heart open and to emanate love. You are to keep your heart clear and block-free, keeping love flowing from you to others, and from others to you.

You are fulfilling the highest potential and we celebrate this moment with a hug, holding you dear and congratulating you for walking the walk of an angel disguised as a human, and so be it.

Knock, Knock

If you hear a knock, and there is no one at the door, you may believe that you imagined the sound, and return to what you were doing. When you hear knocking a second time, you may stay on alert just listening, seeing if it was not again a figment of your imagination. Staying on your sofa, you wait and wait, until a knock comes yet again. This time you have a choice. Opening the door did not work. There was no one there. Waiting and doing nothing did not produce the result you wanted. Now you need to act, but how? You may call the police, you may go yet again and open the door, or you may check yourself into a nearby clinic with the distinct ailment that you hear knocking at the door but there is no one there.

We are knocking on so many doors these days and the response is very similar. You hear the knocking, open the door, but it is the wrong door that you are opening. The knocking is inside of you and the door that you are trying to open is outside of you. No one is coming from the outside. You are looking for the visitor at the wrong entrance. How many times will you try to see who is behind the door, knocking? The more external doors you open, the more inappropriate your response is likely to be. Most of humanity is hearing these knocks; so few are opening the appropriate doors. There is never a judgment and we are here to shine light on your path and allow you to choose. You are conditioned to act, and your response does not align with the new frequency. The door you are asked to open is not accessible by any action on the physical plane. You are asked to open the door leading to the inner sanctuary of your heart.

How do we open this door, you ask? *It's not a physical door.*

Indeed, you sit on your sofa and listen to where the knocking is coming from, to which door of consciousness you are being asked to open. You then open the palms of your hands and gently lay them on the part of your body where the knocking came from. Slowly create an opening with your palms, parting an imaginary veil to allow love to enter. The call to open is there; the knocks are there. Many sit on their sofa watching programs on their TVs or computers and disregard these sounds altogether.

What happens when you act inappropriately or do not hear the knock at all? You will still be sitting on your sofa while a shift so magnificent in scope is happening, and you miss it. What is the purpose, we ask you, of your coming and going? How many times do you need to be reminded that you are not who you think you are? You are beautiful; you are magnificent in every way. The only one who does not recognize your divinity is you, yourself. Your work is to bridge your outer, external story with your inner, internal truth. Opening the door from illusion to truth accesses the path. Each time you hear the knock on the door, it is significant. It gives you the opportunity to shift your awareness from one space to another. There are many sounds to the knocks on your door. A knock can take the form of an accident, an illness, loss of a relative or loved one, a traumatic separation from your lover or child, a divorce, loss of job or income, loss of a home to fire, flood, or foreclosure, depression, or physical ailments that restrict your movements. Each knock is asking you to open a door inside of you.

Why do we tell you about knocks and doors? If we don't we are not fulfilling our mission. Our contract with you is through love. We ask you to remember, and you have the choice; we do not. You hold fears and it is indeed appropriate; you hold anger and hate towards those who wrong you and indeed it has its appropriateness. You hold shame and guilt for being who you are, and indeed it is appropriate. It is your starting point and you have chosen it for a reason. You do not need to know the reason, nor do you need to care. The question of why this is, is not important. The question that you may wish to ask yourself is, "What does this mean to me, and how can I best follow the guidance and move to where I live my truth fully?" Spirit never asks you to be somebody, to prove yourself, to show your divinity, to show your purity, to be the best you can. Spirit does not ask anything of you but to move closer to your light, to live your truth, and by doing so you embody spirit in your totality. That is all. It makes no difference how you are perceived by others, how much income you make, how prestigious your diploma is, what clothes you wear. All you are asked to do on this journey is to remember your divinity and allow it to guide you through this illusion, clearing blocks and opening doors in the process. The deeper you go, the closer you get to your inner God-self. It is not for anyone to reward you for it. It is between you and you to live in your truth.

If there was an angel with wings by your side continually telling you how magnificent you are, how beautiful you are, and whenever you pretend to be someone else, brushes you with her wing asking you, "Why are you doing that? Aren't you enough?" If she then walked with a sign above the head of the person you were speaking with, and the sign read, "You are loved just the way you are. I know who you are, so no need to impress me. Be yourself. You are divinity"; what would you become?

Picture a group of older wise sages with white robes around you, shining their loving smiles, walking with you, escorting you to each meeting you held at your work. Each time you divert from your truth and try to appease the illusion of being someone that you are not, one of them would lift their hand and ask for permission to speak. Of course, you would grant that permission and then with the most beautiful magnificent smile, this sage will ask you: "Who are you doing it for? Don't you see how sacred you are just the way you are? Is this person you are meeting so important that what she feels is more important than your sacred truth?" After the meeting, these sages follow you to your home just for one day. When you get home, they see you wearing a new costume designed for the home theatre. Politely, one of the sages asks permission to speak by raising her hand. She asks gently with a beautiful, soft voice, "You are so divine the way you are, why do you put on this 'funny' costume?" You try to tell her that you meant to make everyone around you happy by doing so, but the look in her eyes knows who you are, and you find yourself at a loss for words. You know that with this group, no excuse will be convincing. At that moment you almost wish you did not grant them permission to speak or to come with you to your workplace and home. For that one day, wherever you are, they follow and remind you that you are sacred just as you are, and you begin to get slightly annoyed by it. Then you go to sleep, and even in your sleep the entourage is with you, holding your hands. Finally, you are too tired to resist, and they take you into a huge arena. All around the arena is light emanating from so many angels. And in the center there is a mattress and someone is sleeping on it. You are given binoculars and when you look closely, it is you on that mattress. Everyone around seems to act in such reverence to the one in the center, and you cannot help but wonder why.

The group is now in your dream sitting all around you. They offer gratitude for your hospitality. They tell you how sacred it is for them to guide you. Each one, in her turn, embraces your sleeping body and gently asks you to remember who you are. With that, they all disappear and leave so you can get some sleep. When you wake up in the morning they are no longer there, and you are so relieved that you can go back to who you were, no angels or sages to embarrass you today or remind you of your divinity. Then you go to work and try to go back to being your old self—the one that is trying to impress and feels inadequate. No angels or sages appear, and again you feel relieved, but then you hear their voices, and the voices seem to come from within you, playing you the melody that was sung the day before. You try to block their voices but whatever you do, these voices are loud and clear, reminding you to be your truth.

You have let spirit in and you can no longer claim that you did not know. Now you have a choice to open the door or leave it shut. This is the awakening we speak of. You no longer require anyone to remind you that you are perfect the way you are. This melody is now stored within you. Walking the walk, imbibing your true melody, living your truth, you emanate light to all. You are a walking lighthouse, illuminating the path of those who come in contact with you. This is why you are here. Your awakening changes Earth and this is your mission now. It's time, and so be it.

Being Alive

When your heart is open, you are one with all that is. You do not need to go anywhere or do anything in particular because you have arrived. We know of your desire to create things in the physical so you could become great. With love, we ask you to open your eyes. You are great and what you create in the physical dimension is an extension of who you are. When you are linked to your heart, you transmit a pulse that is felt all around this universe, and you manifest change based upon love. When you create without residing in your heart, your creation may not support your ascending vibration or that of others. Your role is to be the scaffolding to all those who come in contact with you.

Many of you have said to us, *we are here to serve*, but when it is time to serve, many still say, *this is not the serving I intended or to which I agreed. I wanted it "this" way and I did not think that it would be "that" way.*

"This" or "that" is you placing filters on your eyes and wondering why your picture looks fuzzy. Serving is surrendering to your own higher guidance, and following your own light. Serving is not creating and manifesting, but listening and becoming like a vessel. If you think for a moment that the picture you had in your mind will fit perfectly to your vision, you misunderstood the phrase "to serve".

When you come to Earth and your path has the potential to affect all, you are in service. Service, then, means that you have cleared most of the debris and passed most of the tests that you scheduled for yourself this time around; that you are free of anchors and weight to the extent that just by being, you serve others and your Earth. Being aligned with your purpose is not hard work, as you are being guided at every moment to be in alignment with your purpose. All that comes your way is your guide, and the circumstances in your life are arranged in alignment, supporting your being in every aspect. Whatever blocks still remain within your field are being cleared gently and swiftly as alignment is moving into a groove that is block-free. Reaching the groove and becoming aligned, at times, is hard work. By "hard" we do not mean literally, but metaphorically, since you must move away from the idea of who you are and what your life is about, being ready to adapt to the larger context of being in the physical dimension. Many of you who are in service are yet to find your groove and move into alignment with your true light. You know intuitively that you came here to serve, and you try so hard to be that which you know to be your truth.

For many, though, this service is not altogether satisfying and, from our perch, not fulfilling your "service contract." Becoming one with your purpose is "being." What you actually do is secondary. Being never requires effort. It is doing that requires effort. True service begins when you meet yourself and merge with your heart. True service is being alive, occupying your vessel fully, and vibrating with an open heart to all who cross your path, and many will cross it. The plants and animals know when you are aligned as they respond to the frequency that you emit. People do too, but often they will not recognize the source of the feeling that floods their heart.

Most of you are not as fine-tuned as the natural world around you is, to vibration. A cat will be able to identify a master long before a human could. The plants and insects which come in contact with love respond instantaneously through resonance and they emit the same back to you. We often guide you to be in nature, because nature knows who you are, and it responds to your frequency through biofeedback, supporting your system in miraculous ways. What is asked from you at this time is to be aligned with yourself, nothing more. You do not need to search, because self is already there. You cannot get lost, because you are right, just where you are. You do not need to wander, because you are the wonder. You do not need to prepare because you already have.

What am I to do then, some amusedly ask?

You are to let go of those things which hold you in separation from your light. It is that simple.

How should we do that, you still wonder?

It is only by doing this much, allowing that which comes to guide you and be in tune with the directions offered.

What if I cannot hear anything?

You are being guided, at every moment of your life, to align with yourself. When you do not hear anything, there are two possibilities that we can offer, one is that you are already aligned and whatever you do comes from source. It is, therefore, that you are walking your path. We do, however, suspect that if this is what you are doing, you probably would not ask this question. The other possibility is that there is too much other noise around you that obstructs your hearing. Hearing is a passive sensory receptor that is sensitized by your focused attention. Next time you find yourself wondering if you are being guided and what this guidance offers, find a place in nature beside a tree or a bush, lie on the grass, and allow yourself to let go. Think of nothing. Ask for nothing. You will be astonished at the jewels that are handed to you when you let go of the need to know, and just be.

Why are you speaking to us of service, you ask?

If we had told you that you are loved no matter what you choose, you might be skeptical. If we had told you that being in service is why you came here this time around, you might be skeptical, then, as well. If we tell you that Earth and humanity are waiting for you to align with your truth, so you can lead the way, you might indeed be highly skeptical. But dear angel, this is why you are here, now.

What do you say to the many skeptics who walk their path?

We say to them: "You are loved just as much." Service to Earth is not correcting all the wrongs. What you consider "wrongs" are choices of angels like you, who have not yet opened their eyes to see. The path is different than yours, yet it is honored just as much as yours.

Why is it so, you ask in puzzlement? *I thought I was special and that is why you are with me?*

All angels walking in duality are special, and all have their path of learning. All paths are sacred and divine. When you move by choice to an elevated platform where your vibration is aligned with spirit, embodying your highest potential, the communication is clear, both ways. That which you ask is being heard and that which you need to know is being handed to you in a form you are able to decipher clearly. You are special by choice, as the choices you made affect all vibrationally. That is your specialty and your contract of service. The sum of choices in your universe makes up your human physical dimension. It is therefore not "wrongness" that you see but a simple cause and effect directed by choices. Each angel who chooses to align with their light, walks illuminated and shows the path to those in darkness. This was always the case, but there is more to this story.

Can you tell us the rest of the story, you ask?

The story is simple and profound. Those who came this time around, to illuminate the path for the rest, must begin now. In the scope of your cyclical reality, all must be synchronized to allow movement to be coordinated with celestial bodies, your galactic neighbors, your own evolutionary path. This is the time, now, to become aligned. The forces all around support those of you, who are holding onto the old, to let go, trusting that you will be held and cradled by a safety net. You are asked to let go of your old safety nets, and trust that you will be guided. Being in service to self and Earth, means that you are no longer guided by desires to go somewhere and be attached to outcomes. You allow that which presents itself to you and offer gratitude in an exchange. You move about as if you are using your wings more than your feet. Trust that whatever serves you will appear in your physical dimension to support your path, and whatever is hampering your path must be discarded, making space for the new.

We hear many who say, *that is not true, I am trying and trying but I do not have a way to support myself and nothing I do helps. I need money and it is not coming, so I cannot serve.*

With a smile we ask you to let go, move, explore, play, and live. Do not be attached to your idea of what needs to manifest so you can be "spiritual." Your goal is not to get somewhere, but to be in alignment wherever you end up. Struggling for money and working at a job that is not aligned with who you are, is not our idea of where you need to be.

When you align, your heart knows it, your cells sing that truth, and everything vibrates with alignment around you. To get there, at times, you must let go of all that you consider as plausible, while exploring the implausible. Allow yourself to move to wherever you are called to find yourself. Being fearless on your journey is your only road map. When you let go of your ideas of what you were meant to be doing, you may realize that you are precisely where you were meant to be. All that was needed is a small adjustment in your awareness.

Others may need to move to new territories, or to the other side of the world, just so they can be released from preconceived ideas of who they are and align with their authentic self. This is what you are being asked to do and be. The integration of your inner aspect with your outer aspect is the healing. When you do this, your resonance is heard throughout all dimensions and you are in service.

For you to correct all the "wrongs" on Earth, means that you must give up "free will." There is nothing actually "wrong" in the picture humanity painted for itself. What you see is your free will manifested, and the picture reflects your collective choices. The most profound contribution you can gift Earth is being aligned with your own light, vibrating from your heart. It is the place where each human is connected to every other human, and when the melody of the heart is playing, all the potentials are now supported from the vibration of the heart. You are allowing all the choices now being selected to pass through the heart portal—your own, and others who resonate with high frequency. You have placed a protective shield around Earth, which guides each of the trillion possibilities to manifest the one, which is heart-based. This is your call to service. The time is now, and so be it.

The Difference Between A Human and An Angel

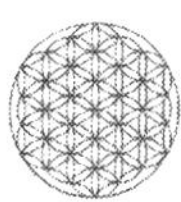

What is the difference between a human and an angel, you ask?

A human is an angel in training, we say with a smile. An angel is a frequency, a vibration of love. When a human has reached such a vibration, they fully embody the energy of an angel. If we had to guess what the rate is of humans becoming angels, we must say it is too slow. However, this is changing now.

Why is it changing, you inquire?

When a human is touched by an angel, he or she is forever transformed. When a human is touched by another human through love he or she is forever transformed. Love transforms you; it melts even a rock into sediments light enough to flow with water. Love is not only the substance that flows between two humans in love. Love is you expanding the idea of who you are and linking continually with your higher aspect, which is the "I am." Your expanded self sees, hears, smells, and touches using your senses, but the melody it hears is different, the taste is different, the touch is different. The senses are those of a human, but the perception is that of an angel. You are not who you think you are. It is a joke to many that we speak of the angel in the human, but human is just a temporary role you play and indeed it is a sacred role. You come to a place that has you torn between so many choices, at any given moment, and you somehow are miraculously expected to know which choice brings more light?

Many of you are now seeing yourselves in your expanded roles and you are becoming uneasy about what you see. Some of you even think that there is something wrong with yourself. It is because you wake up in the morning one way, and when you are ready to go to sleep after a long and challenging day you are different. Something happened along the way. You have changed. What is this change you feel? The answer is, you became infected by love. When the vibration enters your cells and takes hold, your cells link with the universal symphony all around you and you expand, seemingly, overnight.

How can I tell the difference between the "infected" ones and the "uninfected" ones, you ask?

The answer is easy, you fall in love with the infected ones, you want to take them home with you and make them your own. You want to tie yourself to the one infected because you wish to intravenously receive what they have. You want to reside in their heart and be nourished by their light. It may prove difficult because angels are frequency messengers. Their role is to infect you with what they have so you can develop along that path. They are not meant to be holding your hands and taking you along but activating your own source of love, pointing their hands to the direction higher, and nudging you to walk, knowing that you are safe and loved. It is your time now to become a full-fledged angel by claiming your heart and being a messenger of the most precious and powerful vibration in your universe—love.

More of you are now becoming activated humans and, as you move around and touch others, you infect them with love. Your resonance is infectious. When you touch a soul with your infectious light, that soul is forever changed.

What makes my life so precious, you wish to know?

The sacredness of your journey, and the potential to transform, we say.

You speak in riddles, some may complain.

We speak to your cells, we answer with a smile. Our dance with you is through love, and we do not need to explain it as your left brain is already overworked as it is. You need to feel your heart, and when you feel linked to your heartbeat, you act as a conduit of love. It is impossible to be in the heart and to cause harm. It is impossible to be in the heart at the same time that you are being judgmental.

When you feel your heart, you are connecting to the greater love field that is around you. The reason you are here is to activate latent memory within your cellular structure, which will begin a chain reaction. That chain reaction is a dance that we call sacred and, in effect, it is an alignment of the various aspects of your "I am." The alignment is a by-product of your activation. Your path clears itself from barriers and obstacles, your body aligns with a more harmonious melody, your heart opens to love, and your awareness expands to include the larger aspect of you, the "I am." Each human that turns angel changes the balance of light and dark on your planet. When you walk by an angel, you may not see the wings, and you may not notice a halo, but you will surely feel love surging in your veins. Falling in love with an angel is like falling in love with yourself, just now you have become aware that they are an extended you. People may come into your life, and you may feel their light, see their inner beauty, delve into their clarity and purity. You may feel these things so much so that you wish to chain the angel to yourself so you will have access to all that vibration. Dear human, this is not how it works; an angel is a domain that mixes with a human via frequency and not via building a home. If you are adamant that you wish to take an angel home, you will turn her earthbound. When you see a beautiful butterfly, you wish to hold it in your hands and celebrate its joy and beauty, know that when you do their delicate powder rubs off their wings and they can no longer fly. Allow them to fly and rejoice in their existence. Angels stay in the realm of high vibrations, facilitate when needed, direct when needed, open your heart, and guide you to open your own doors. When a human turns angel they take on a larger role, the role of a healer in a planetary sense. Any movement is being recorded because it affects the multitudes. When you meet the angel, smile and let them know that you are grateful. Not that they need to hear it, but it is an acknowledgment of this sacred reunion. It is how the above is linked to the below through those who carry higher vibrations acting as conduits.

Why are you speaking to us about human angels, you ask?

Because you are one, and we ask you to know your role and find peace with it. When you have completed your work here on Earth, you may go back to our dimension and facilitate work from there. There is never rest from where we come from, but it does not feel like work because it is a labor of love. Your other option is to remain on Earth but take on a different role. In your spiritual writings you call it "ascension." Each time you chose light over darkness your vibration ascends. When you reach a melody that is harmonious with a universal love frequency, you grow wings. With your new wings you can fly. As you soar above your reality and observe all that is taking place from above, you are in a detached place where the day to day does not carry the same weight for you. You see it from a bird's eye and it no longer seems so daunting or threatening. From above everything seems smaller and placed where it should be. When you spread your wings and become airborne, what seemed to be out of place is no longer so. You find yourself soaring and loving. In whatever shape or form you interact with people they are touched by your melody and can briefly see through your expanded energy the larger context of their reality.

Why do you tell us all that and why now?

It is time. More of you are growing wings. You find it challenging to reconcile this reality with your new reality and you feel that something may be wrong. With all love we wish to reassure you that nothing is wrong. The path you are on is sacred and revered by all. Your role is to be a bridge. A bridge must have firm footings on both banks of the river, so those who walk on it can pass safely. This is your expanded role, to lead those who choose to ascend to cross this bridge. Some will want to hang on you, the bridge, and remain in the middle. You are a conduit and you are love; your role is to awaken and ignite the memory of others to their own potential. You have chosen to walk, and we walk with you, everyday along your path.

What makes this journey worthwhile, your left-brain inquires?

Your universal yearning is to expand light in the universe of free choice. A human, who turns angel, plants seeds of light everywhere she sets foot. As she walks, people's hearts open, hands that were clutched surrender, and eyes that were shut closed begin to sparkle. The vibration emanating from a meeting between the one who embodies love and the one who opens her heart to love is like a reunion of twin souls. They merge, and both are changed forever. Love expands and light illuminates. Your role is to be a bridge, a conduit, a lover, and to allow that which crosses your path to touch your heart, without having your heart change colors. You are a vibration, a melody, a frequency, which manifests in form. When you begin to dance to the melody of universal love, you hold the space for all those who came here to light their flames and illuminate Earth.

What is the purpose of all this, your left-brain inquires unsatisfied?

You exist in a vast reality, much larger than you can ever fathom with your senses. If you had access to a multi-sensory perception sensitive to a wider range of frequency, you would be exposed to some of the activity that is taking place around you.

You emerge from the birth canal of your mother, within a short time you are an adult, and then it is time to go back home. What do you think is the purpose for such a journey? Do you believe that it is to make money, or to marry well? Do you believe it is to have a family, or to find a good job? Do you even believe that it may be to find God?

That last one is angelic humor, as you are God. So many of you are on a desperate search to find God and all along that God is hiding inside of you waiting to be acknowledged.

So what is going on, you ask?

You are a messenger of light to a reality that is still permeated in darkness and pain. You are here to transform dark to light and allow others to remember who they really are. Your role is simple, create light and ascend. You choose a script, a storyline, a set design, which encompasses your parents, relatives, country, and the place you were born to, genetic predispositions, economic and cultural set design, ethnic heritage, then off you go. Now it is on you to take all these colors and mix them well to create your own hues, learn to use a brush, a palette, your fingers, your toes, and whatever tools you have to apply these colors on your canvas. As you apply, you create, and as you create, you transform what was to what is and what will be. You are the creator from day one, but along your path some of you begin to remember and apply all that you have learned, yet forgotten, to your canvas. The time is now to awaken to why you are here. Your light is not in the money you make, nor is it hidden in the car that you drive, or your diplomas. Your light is hidden in your heart, and each time you open your heart, light pours out and adds illumination to where there was none. Your choices, thoughts, feelings, and actions are the basis for your vibration.

Like a violin, the pressure of your touch, pulling on the strings, and stroking the strings with the bow is how you create music. We walk with you and help you remember. Once you remember you awaken your heart and emit a melody that awakens others. Your planet's rate of human-turning angels is accelerating now, and we are in awe of your work. All that we say you already know, but one thing.

What may that one thing be, you ask curiously?

It is that you are not whom you think you are. You are us and we are you. When we merge, we are God, and so be it.

Nothing and Everything

Grateful I am, for this journey.

Beautiful you are. As the sun rises from the east, everything that was in darkness is illuminated. This is the way of it. As the world turns, darkness is replaced by light. As you walk, the Earth turns, and circumstances change. Where darkness once reined, light is now in abundance. All of you have opportunities throughout your journey to crack the darkness and let light in. You are a human, yet you are not, you are an angel, yet you are not, you are galactic, yet you aren't, you live and die, yet you don't, you exist in time and space, yet you do not. You are individual, yet you aren't, you are one, yet you are not. You are fragmented, yet you aren't. You experience pain, you experience pleasure, you experience joy, and you experience agony, you create and you destroy, you love and you hate, you take and you give. You are beautiful, because you are nothing and everything simultaneously. You are vast, yet you are insignificantly small. You are able to embody the lightest of angels and the darkest of monsters. Who are you then? What are you then? Where are you coming from and where are you going to? You come from nowhere and you are going nowhere. You are the great "I am." You come solely for the purpose of experiencing a choice in the midst of forgetfulness and your aim is to remember. You create and destroy for the purpose of finding balance. You act externally until you realize that no such thing exists, and all is inside of you. You explore the vastness of existence so you can grow, and the purpose of your growing is to become one with self and with all that is. Your aim is to merge with the true essence of self which is expressed in everything. Everyone around you is an aspect of you, all your accomplishments, your treasures, as well; your creations are an aspect of your journey to define yourself because without creating in the physical dimension you have difficulty seeing who you are. We are here to illuminate your mirror, so you can better see your silhouette. Then, from the shadow of your self, infer the light; from the depth down below, infer your height, and from the darkest of the dark, infer your illumination. You are a mystery and you hold within you the code to the vastness of existence, yet many live in a reality that is constrained by fear, pain, and ego, to see only what is in front of them. Yes, you are an enigma, to yourself and to us. We often are puzzled how you do not see your power, your sacredness, your divinity, your connectedness to all that is. We often shed angelic tears when you move into the character of the victim, buying into the story that you have no power and that your slate in this lifetime is somehow robbed of opportunities and light, leaving you only with a little bit of gray to get you by. Yes, you are an enigma and we love you for it. You are an enigma to all the light beings roaming your universe and they, like us, do not understand how you do not see who you are. You have the potential at any given moment to see, but most choose not to open their eyes.

We ask why, yet we know the answer. This is your journey and sacred it is. You come here not to find answers, but to live the question. You came here not to become, but to be. All the secrets that you came here to discover are hidden in your heart. Many feel that they want to solve the mysteries. Humans go through incredible lengths to crack open the secrets to your universe. Your scientists feel that they are somehow getting closer to solving the mysteries, yet the ones who are, in fact, solving the puzzles are not your scientists, but those who expand themselves to include all within their beingness. You do not read about them in your journals, nor see them on your television screens. They do not seek approval, nor do they need recognition. They do not need safety, nor do they ask questions. They live their questions and rejoice in the enigma of existence. They experience highs and lows, explore light and darkness while, at the poles of each extreme, their smile remains at the forefront, because being is different than becoming, asking, different than knowing. You try to figure out who you are and what your purpose is. Your search is sacred.

The answer seems to be at hand at different junctures, yet, with an angelic smile, we tell you that you can never find a definitive answer to your pursuits. Each answer comes in time just to be rebuffed by a new question. You are a reality creator and each time you master one reality a new door opens to show you there is no such thing as definitive reality. All is your creation, and all is in constant flux. Those of you who hold a definitive persuasion that they have the answers are those who stop growing. Your reality is determined by your vantage point at any given moment on this journey. Your perceived limitations are also your gifts. You are forced to explore your vastness each time a limit is placed upon you. If all would be wide open, how would you learn about your powers? If you had all the answers, when would you seek questions? If your reality acted in a linear, logical, and predictable way, why would you explore your true identity, searching for the laws that govern existence? You are never far from your truth, and you are never far from your light. At the same moment, you are, as well, never far from the question, and you are never far from your mystery.

Your role now is to be present to the movement that is raging around you and to see through it all, piercing the veil. Your role is to embrace the mystery without holding on to anything. When you are given a baton and an orchestra, you must infer that you are the conductor. When you move your hand in an erratic manner, the sounds coming out from the orchestra chamber may make you cringe, and some of you still wonder why. You hold the baton and we ask you to begin with a question. The question is aimed at self. Why do I create a sound that is less than harmonious? You learn through feedback as most cannot see into their own mystery. You send a vibration out into the world and, like a bat that can sense the echo to its own sound, you receive a response from your vibration in a form of your reality. This is how you learn, but most do not make the connection between the vibration they create and the reality that is seemingly created around them. You feel that there is no correlation, that this is your lot in life and some arbitrarily get more, and others get less. More or less is your human way of defining self and others, but to us you are all one, each exploring her own aspect of the one. None of you are here by mistake. Each fragment is essential to the wholeness of the one. None is more or less essential than the other. Each one of you plays their role, but the role is not you. The more you realize your oneness, the more harmonious the melody emanating from your orchestra.

What is it that I am asked to do and be this lifetime, some ask?

Two words, *let go*, is our answer. Let go of who you think you should become, let go of your idea of limitation, let go of your inadequacies, let go of your ideas of good and bad, let go of separation. Let go of anything onto which you previously held. Let go of fears, let go of wanting, let go of any idea about who you are or what you are.

Letting go creates space within you to expand, grow, explore, and become light, so you can fly. Allow your self to re-invent you. Make space and clear clutter. Allow whatever holds you back to be released. This advice is somewhat misleading because even if you try to hold on, your attempts are likely to be fruitless. It is however always less challenging when you consciously choose, rather than being forced to let go. It is December of 2012, and the galactic needle is now aligned to support your own alignment. You are part of your universe and it's time for you to play your role. Loved you are, sacred you are, beautiful you are and, whatever you may choose, your choice is always honored above all. We came to you five years ago and introduced to you the first message that spoke about your choices. We have sat beside you at the exact place you are sitting today and placed our wings around your fragile frame charging you with love and filling your heart with light. We asked you on that day to choose and you have chosen at each juncture to embrace light and let go of darkness. You are so dearly loved for being and walking the sacred walk of an angel in human costume.

You are now stepping into your expanded role as each of you is called to hold their own baton and play their melody harmoniously in this planetary orchestra.

Where am I going, you ask?

Nowhere, we answer with a smile. You are staying where you are; it is your awareness that is shifting, your cells expanding, and your light growing. Within the limitation of your physical frame, you are connecting all the doing to the universal symphony playing all around you, tying each string with love, as the strings, vibrating their resonance, move the next one and the next one, so that you are taking part in this game of life, affecting all.

You have been given a key and the lock now opens. Each of you carries a key on their heart and that key opens the chambers to the mysteries now unfolding. We ask you to let go of your heaviness and open the palms of your hands so space will be created within you to dance. Many are shaken by losing so many things and having less and less. With all love we ask you not to replace heaviness with heaviness. There is a purpose for all this shedding, it makes you lighter and creates inner space for the new to replace the old. Do not resist what is to come, but embrace each day with a question, asking, where am I to be in my power playing the most harmonious melody and shining my light? Now move to the battlefield where you will be pushed and shoved, scratched and beaten at times. Know that it is just a phase, an initiation to move from heavy to light. You are being initiated and crowned with your power. Be still and observe, do not let drama sideswipe you, and do not allow fear to freeze your dance. It is the time for Earth to move into a sacred dance and it is your music that inspires this dance. Sacred it is. With tears of joy we are now saying goodbye, yet we are never too far. We ask you to be that which you are, an angel moving through a human experience rippling music that awaken others, allowing them to view their own reality from a new perspective, so owning their power and light.

You are all renegades who came to break the locks, releasing the codes of love, light, and the self-empowerment of "I am," re-linking those who are lost back to their home. You are one of torch holders and, with reverence, we ask you to know who you are. And so be it.

The Sphinx

Wherever you are, you are loved. The sphinx is your guide as it holds many secrets within its being, yet it does not divulge these secrets. Only those who can decipher the codes of the sphinx are allowed entry into the mysteries.

Why is it so, you may ask? *Why not reveal the mysteries to the whole wide world and have everyone explore these revelations?*

When you are a three-year-old toddler and you are shown a movie meant for adults, how can the young mind interpret the visual stimuli that are projected to it. Naturally, she has yet to develop her vocabulary to decipher these signals.

Will she suffer harm by watching, some would inquire? *Would those who are not ready for the mysteries get hurt by being exposed prematurely?*

A toddler who is watching a movie meant for an adult is most likely to have an inappropriate emotional reaction to what she sees. It is the way of it. Most of humanity are in the toddler stage and do not possess the tools needed to process knowledge of the mysteries. It may not necessarily harm, but it surely would have no benefit. It could however provoke an inappropriate response that could hurt the person exposed.

Confusion, fear, anxiety, panic, depression, or overreaction are some of the inappropriate responses we have observed in those who are not yet ripe to receive yet were exposed to the mysteries. So many of you wish to know the mysteries. It is not the knowing that is crucial to your advancement, but your experiences. Your mind may know, but for you to move forward your heart needs to know. Your initiation is your actual physical experiences and your reaction to those experiences. You possess natural curiosity and a passion to explore. It is in your genetic makeup and is the power behind your movement to grow and mature. The mysteries test your heart, not your mind. Your heart carries the codes to the ultimate combination, opening the doors to the mysteries.

What are these mysteries, and why do we really need to care, some may ask?

When you chose to explore a cave looking for a treasure, you are determined to go all the way until you discover that treasure. You are all explorers and you come here to explore self in relation to everything else around you. May it be your lover, your enemy, the Earth, the planets, the elements and the natural world, the cosmos and the universe, all are part of you. Your exploration is fueled by your yearning to know who you are. At times it is through going inside and at times it is achieved through exploring your placement within all that is around you. All paths are sacred and revered. Ancient knowledge was kept in vaults and hidden in codes to protect you from you. Those who were present at the time had access to portals of the past and gateways into the future. Many could see the direction and outcome of a process, which started eons ago. The sages of the past did not have your modern technology, but they had access to the workings of the mysteries and could retrieve that information at will. They knew that premature exposure was not in line with the universal laws. They knew that all physical reality is an expression of laws. They knew that a fruit requires its "time" to ripen, and a flower to blossom. There was no judgment as to how quick or how slow one's movement was within the cycle. There was always a right time and it was always accurate.

Your ancestors knew that there is no rush to get anywhere. They held sacred that all movements are but an expression of a flow back and forth within a sphere. All that goes up must come down and all that sways to the left must also sway to the right. Their main ambition was to be aligned with the universal flow that was manifested all around their physical reality. Unlike you, they wanted to read the map and walk in alignment with the charted path. You are, at the moment, out of balance with the universal flow, as you have veered from the path of reading the map, and you are attempting to force your will on the universal laws around you. The universal laws always maintain a desire for equilibrium, so, whenever there is a powerful movement out of balance in one direction, it will stretch until it reaches its limit and then it will reverse its direction with equal force. None in the universe can act outside these laws. No beings of light, angels, or God can be outside these laws. You are beautiful to us and when you are misguided by your desires you are still beautiful. When you move out of balance to the left, no matter how far off the path you veered, we know that at some point you will re-track to the right in order to reach balance. This is the way of it. When you choose to go deep into the cave of mysteries, many sights present themselves to you. Your interpretation of these sites is your key to opening gates. In many sites around your Earth clues were placed in centers of energy, which were designed to allow you access to the greater story of you. Each of these sites is an aspect of the greater story of you and therefore corresponds to an aspect of the self. The keys to unlock each of these sacred sites, is to feel to which element of the self they correspond. Follow these keys by exploring the function of the corresponding aspect of your body on your well-being and physical equilibrium. You have moved to a wider arena and there is no single path more energized than another. The field is open. Many of you know this intuitively and the tug of war rages on, left or right, up or down, dark or light. For you, the one who chose to be here at this time, you came to play a role. Your role is to awaken your own keys and to self-balance that which has moved away from balance and align that which veered from alignment.

How then can all be working for the same goal, you may ask? *Why not ask all to help?*

With a hug, there is a role for each one of you like there is a role for the sun, the moon, gravity, and the different elements. If there would be only air but no water, life on Earth would not be possible. There is a place for left and right, for minus and plus, dark or light.

We ask you to awaken to your own knowing that your role is to discover the mysteries of self, and bring light to where there was only dark before. We follow you wherever you are, guiding, loving, hugging. It is this knowing which may allow you, at times, to delve into the pain of your heart and into darkness that never before felt possible. Some wonder why, with all this love, the pain grows larger and more intense. When you know that you are loved and never judged; when you know that you are protected; when you know that you are eternal, you are able to go into the gate of the abyss and face yourself. Some of you who have traveled extensively along their path are now facing the most challenging tests.

You wonder, *why work so hard, if, in the end I only face more challenges?*

You are only faced with that which you are able to handle, thereby fulfilling the reason you came here. To some the challenges of now are the fruits of lifetimes of explorations. Like the mysteries, you must face your own darkness and it is presented to you when you are ready. Some, who seemingly have it easier, may not be ready to face that which is more intense.

Must we face these dark sights, you ask?

You must face yourself, whether it is dark or light. Through yourself, you affect all. When you look around, some may see the work that needs to be done. Much seems to be out of balance. How do you believe this work is done, we ask with a smile? As above, so below is how you affect all. You are your universe. When you create a change in the physical landscape it is sacred, but when you change internally, you change all.

The forces that are swirling all around you are your guides. You must find your own alignment with these forces. You have come from the far reaches of the universe to embody energy with the purpose of rippling new reality into the fabric of Earth's dimension.

How is that being done, you ask? *Do we need to know the mysteries?*

The mysteries will be revealed to you when you are ready. Many of you explore deeply the writings and words of sages. It is sacred to understand, yet the mysteries cannot be understood with your mind. As you spread your wings and move from your limited four dimensions to all dimensions, no words exist in your vocabulary to describe what it is that you feel. Any attempt will only diminish the story. We wish you, therefore, to open yourself to the mysteries, but do not pursue them. Know that the sphinx will speak when you are ready to hear what it holds in store for you.

You have just experienced moving through the portal gate of December 21st, 2012, and the world seemingly has not changed; yet to those of you who understand the mysteries, everything changed. In the passage of time, physical reality ripples in a predictable way dictated by the causes that have preceded the effects. You have moved through a gate in a space–time sphere where all the possibilities are open. Some of the old rules no longer apply and each wave of energy carries a potency that is affecting all. It is a time like no other and we have told you over the past four years to prepare yourself for this time. It is a time for celebration and a time to use all your tools to align with your purpose. Your story has always been greater than anyone could ever imagine. The work ahead of you is to embody the fullness of your power and become attuned to the whispers all around you. Move with the whispers, become subtle, become sensitive, become light, become a conduit for love to ripple through all. Imbibe all you know and create a fire, so to dispel the dark, burning up that which no longer serves. Know that you are so dearly loved and what you do affects all that you see. Do not look for proofs outside of yourself. There will be jolts and tremors, push and pull, carrying higher intensities as the core balance is being tossed looking for its center. Be the center and hold onto your light. This ride is as exciting as it gets and the reason you are here. The mysteries are rippling from places where ancient cultures left clues as to your potential and your greater story. Know that you are dearly loved and supported at this time, to move deeper than you ever did. All that you know is changing and you are at the forefront of this change. There is no longer a need to seek explanations and culprits behind all the wrongs you perceive out in the world. You now know that all you see is part of you and your contract reads that you shine no matter what darkness presents itself on your path. We wish you to ignite the light in you and shine, knowing that it is the reason you are now here, and so be it.

Limbo

Even now when you see that which is in front of you, do you still embrace it as truth? If anyone ever took your hand down a dark path and told you to close your eyes and follow their lead, would you follow? Do you finally see that what appears to be one may also be another? Light is only light, but dark can have many shades. How certain are you that you indeed follow the light?

How do we really know? You ask.

There is one way only to be certain we say with a smile. You must connect to your heart, close your eyes, and ask your heart to show you the truth. When you ask your heart with pure intent it will always show you your truth. We are asking you to be in your heart because when you reside in your heart, there is no duality, no darkness, no shadows, no questions. We say over and over again do not be dissuaded by sweet words or words of fear. Look inside and consult your pulse. Your truth speaks to you from inside. When you listen, you know. If you are still confused, become still. Listen, then, more attentively until you receive the answer. Do not always listen to the one who is the loudest. Often love is quiet and subtle. It embraces you without conditions and it whispers. When you are connected to your heart you are fully protected from deceit and manipulations. You are protected from the dark, because dark cannot enter where it is lit. It is a cosmic law that all must adhere to in all dimensions, and it is why we ask you to commit to living from your heart.

Take pause and look back. What do you see? We have been guiding you with light to where you needed to be to create ripples and openings for new energy to enter and replace what was.

How do I know that anything did change? You ask us often. *I want proof,* you say. *I want to see that change.*

Yes, we know, and it may take some time to see the full effect of the change. What you can see are seedlings taking root. The seedlings don't look like the old vegetation. They seem to be greener than ever before.

I wish to see something concrete, you say, frustrated.

Whenever there is a vast movement, which incorporates all aspects of your life, you will see the change only in a reflection at first. What we mean is that life, reflected back to you, will, at first, feel different. As if the colors of your reality have been enhanced and a new melody has been synthesized. The motions and movements are seemingly the same but are reflected back to you differently than before. Fears that you had, by now, showed up so you could face them and move beyond them. Relationships that were not aligned, by now, have fallen apart or are in the process of doing so. Dreams that many have held in a file called "someday," tucked away in the back of your file cabinet, are now being dusted off and moved to the front of the pile. Aspects of your life, which were not moving anywhere, have shifted, and now, for many, you have more questions than answers. It is a time of limbo. What many are experiencing now is a sensation of fluidity, as if there is no longer such a thing as truth and no longer any real knowing, as all is in a state of flux.

Why so, you ask?

You are in an accelerated dimension now. Not only are all the processes around your reality accelerated, but you are no longer traveling in a set groove. The playfield is vast and the destination is guided by your choice and intent. You are in control now. Your choice is your campus as the groove that was there to guide you for millennia is no longer. The playing field is now wide open. The portal of December 21st, 2012, opened up as scheduled, as well as other energy gateways for the past five years. The changes that were introduced to you through each gate created a movement that can no longer be contained nor controlled in the same way that it was.

The grooves have been overrun by the water. It could be compared to a flood. As the water rises, it must go somewhere. The water has swelled above all the barriers and now is flowing to where it is guided by the terrain. The swelling happened as more and more of you opened your heart valves and allowed more "liquid light" to flow through. Many of you have been going places and exploring different venues for growth, venues, which appeared to you seemingly from nowhere and have become, almost overnight, part of your life. These new venues are the reflections of which we speak. You see the changes in your life through the changes you observe in your outer reality. Have you noticed any changes?

Since your year of 2007 you have been on an accelerated journey clearing lifetimes, often in a matter of hours. Initiations that were meant to be a life lesson became short occurrences and then you moved on. You have plowed through many difficult moments and stayed with the light.

How do I bridge my life before with my now reality, you ask?

The world, as you know it to be, has changed its rhythm and it no longer spins the same way. You have entered a zone of electromagnetic storm that is brewing and forming from within Gaia. This storm will show itself to you in the form of immense movements of particles from one polarity to the other extreme polarity. Like a lightning storm, an immense charge is being generated which must find outlets in order for the energy to discharge. We have asked you over and over to slow down and to teach yourself to contain energy so you will be ready. Your subtle bodies, which used to spin at one rate, are now spinning twice as fast. You are surely being challenged to stay in a place of balance. The fluctuations of highs and lows can cause even a seasoned seaman to become nauseated. The particles charging you through your sun create a stronger polarity inside your being. In essence, it is as if a battery is being charged to overcapacity. It is no wonder that you witness more human angels snapping and losing control, expressed at times as horrific acts of violence. Some events become conduits for the discharge of this immense energetic polarity that now exists.

On the other side of this polarity, sacred and divine acts of benevolence are now being initiated, creating immense luminosity that moves like waves rippling, invoking compassion and love around your planet.

How do I handle this charge, you ask?

You learn to breathe deeply, become still, and, at the same time, surrender to the powerful charge moving through you. The movement, at times, feels light, and, at other times, will feel heavy, but it is just a movement. It cannot be called light nor can it be called dark. It is a storm. You cannot call a storm light or dark. It is a movement, and you can only hold on to your own balance, not resisting this storm or running away from it. Your body, which was used to work metaphorically on 110 volts, is now being plugged into a charge closer to 220 volts. This can cause you to be ground up and to snap faster, and with greater intensity than before.

Many of you expected bells and whistles to come at this time, yet what you were told all along is that reality is changing so that different elements of your life must be aligned in order to remain intact. These elements within one's reality, not a part of your path, are being dislodged, discarded like old rugs. There is not enough gravitational force to hold on to what does not belong to you. 2012 is the end of a story and a beginning of a new one. Open your notebook and begin to write a new chapter, this one more glorious and more exciting than we could ever anticipate.

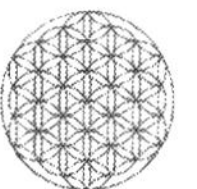

The darkness that you see is what must be expelled from you and transformed to love.

We have asked you over and over again to look inside because the only source of pure light is emanating from your heart. Love is all there is. Life, as you know it, has changed and will continue changing. You are at the forefront of a movement upward. There is no stopping!

We ask you to look at yourself in the mirror and ask your reflection, who am I? What am I doing here? Where am I going? You have delved deeply into the cavern of your souls on a search to find your truth, your light. We have told you that, by changing yourself you change all. We have told you that you have asked to be here now. We have told you that you came here to chart a new path so others can follow. Yes, you are a leader whether you like it or not. Each one of you, who chooses to be in your center, keeping your torch lit above their head, is crowned as a leader. As a leader, many may follow your example. We asked you to walk quietly and to remain still. We asked you to do less and be more. We asked you to live from your heart. We have seen that those of you who are riding on hot air balloons will be coming to a time when those balloons deflate, descending back to where they began.

We ask you to ride the spiral of light emanating from your heart core. No need to use any vehicles except your multidimensional wings which all of you have.

What is it that I am doing here, you ask yourself?

The time has come for you to recognize fully who you are. You are a human angel playing two roles simultaneously. Introduce yourself all over again. Take your meditation scarf with you and open it. Place it on the floor. Cross your legs and sit on it.

Take the palms of your hands and place them on your heart, left hand first, look to the east and say, "I am blessed."

Then, turn to the west and say, "I am divine."

Turn to the north and say, "I am that I am."

Finally, turn to the south and say, "I am love, I am loved, from love I come and to love I return."

For every time that you feel darkness, know that you are making space for light. Each time you take a leap not knowing if you'll end up at the bottom of a pit never to be found again, or lying on a bed of roses, know that you have moved in alignment with your role. You must move, change, create, explore, open, and open some more. Then, when you feel that you can no longer open because you will fall apart and become discombobulated, you are asked to trust and open some more. When you feel that metaphorically you have reached the edge of a cliff and there is no more safe space for you to progress, we ask you to take the next step. This is what is being asked from you.

Do you wish us to crash and die? Some ask.

We ask you to trust your wings and know that there is no darkness out there, or threat that can come to you, when you are in your heart, unless you intentionally invite it in. Yes, you are asked to test your power and step into it all the time. Test your limits and discover that there are no limits only limitations.

What if I lose everything, you ask?

Then you have gained everything is our answer. All that you lose, ever, is your hold on being attached to your limitations. When you let go of limitations, the concept of losing vanishes. What is disappears because it always was and always will be an illusion. On your path there is no loss, only gain, there is only light, no darkness, but, at times, to gain you must lose and to go to the light you must pass through darkness. At the point where you believe that you have lost everything and there is nothing left, you move into the treasure, discovering the "I am." You can never lose the "I am." It is your divine birthright and all else is a set design; a context to advance on your journey. Feel the elements: the air, the fire, the water, the wind, and the earth. You are made of these elements so you can become one with all that is. To become one, you need to let go of what separates you from becoming one, which is fear. The more you are willing to risk the more you may gain. When you finally discover that in actuality you did not risk anything and there was only upside, many begin to fathom the grandness of this journey. Those places on Earth, which used to hold you anchored in the reality of gravity, are all, vibrating with a new melody. This melody has released you from your chains. You are free, but you have yet to realize it. Like a giant elephant tied to a small branch yet unable to move freely. Since birth the young elephant was tied to an enormous tree and it was conditioned that it can never move away from it. Now the elephant grew larger and the tree reduced, almost to the size of a twig, yet the elephant will not try to break away from it. Like the elephant, your conditioning was so strong that you have always believed that you cannot break free so many do not even try. We ask you to try. Make a move and see what happens. Your one certainty on this journey is that change is a constant. Everything moves, vibrates, oscillates, and shifts. Become one with the law of vibration, harmonized with the melody now being heard all over your dimension. Wherever you are and whatever you do on this journey, your role is the same, to become one with self and to harmonize with the energy now permeating your Earth, supporting it, so to allow Earth to find its equilibrium with the human angels, its inhabitants. Your role is sacred and so are you, and so be it.

Lost Innocence

When the skies are gray, remember that there is still a sun shining above the clouds. We wish to check with you today and guide you to re-discover your lost innocence, the child that was once you and now is in hiding. We wish to take this child by the hand and reassure this child that it is safe to come out from her bunker. We wish to have this child feel safe again.

A purity of heart always resides in the mind of the child. The laughter of a child is the most healing sound in the universe. If you listen to it long enough, you will be free from all worries. It will heal all ailments; you will become aligned with the universal joy that is your birthright. The laughter of a child is the antidote to all maladies. The stream of life is pure when it comes out of its source in the belly of Gaia, but, as it flows through valleys and mountains it collects all kinds of residues from the surroundings and becomes a carrier of its surroundings to the oceans.

So are you. As you emerge from source you are pure and your laughter is pure. As you interact with other humans, like the stream, you collect the impressions from your surroundings, taking them with you, becoming you. Your journey is about merging and when you finally become one with the ocean, all that you have collected throughout your life enriches the whole. The purity of your original self is always there but it is mixed with all the substances and residues you collect.

How do you access your pure self? Where does it reside, you may wish to know?

You can access it in your dream state.

How?

Ask for it. Give intent before you close your eyes. Ask to remember what it felt like to be a child, to laugh carefree, to feel the fullness of your body before guilt and shame became part of your stream. Ask to feel the hugs of your mother and father as a baby, when you were surrendered and helpless, but, oh, so aware. You came awakened and you fell asleep. That is your agreement, to come fully awake, to forget; then to try to remember again your purpose and your divinity. To once again link with whom you are, and what the pure version of you feels like. When a stream passes through vast distances it collects minerals, depositing them, distributing them, wherever it goes, nourishing all life. Life without mineralized water is not sustainable.

You are the representative of the consciousness of Gaia and as you become enriched with deposits, you enrich the whole. When a child plays with mud, it is often with great joy. Only when the child comes home, when the parent may scold her for getting her clothes dirty and wet, will the child begin filtering away the pure joy through the perceived misbehavior, to keep that parent from yelling. Since birth you are directed to move away from being carefree while learning control and rules. This journey is appropriate and by design. It allows you to function in a society and learn boundaries, which support your journey as a human. Then there is a time as you ascend and climb the steep mountainous trails of spiritual terrain that you must begin to decipher the difference between the pure version of you, and what was "gifted to you" by others.

It is time, now, to link with the purity of the child you once were. It is essential to connect with the pure heart of carefree laughter. It is sacred to look again at your body like an infant discovering her toes for the first time. When you were little, all aspects of your body were equally sacred and you were just beginning to learn what is yours and what is not. You had yet to place a judgment on good, bad, appropriate, or inappropriate. We ask you to find that space in you again. Not that you need to behave like an infant, but recall what it felt like to be holy from head to toe. So much darkness will be expelled from you in the process. Waves of hurt, shame, or excruciating pain must, at times, be dislodged for you to re-experience the pure self of the "I am." Many have worked hard throughout your journey on Earth to design strategies of survival, mechanisms for coping, so you will be accepted and be perceived by your environment as good. When you were fresh out of the birth canal, you had no such worries. You knew that you are here and a piece of divinity. Making contact with the pure version of you requires strength. At times you are asked simultaneously to both mourn whom you were and celebrate whom you have become despite of your circumstances. Shedding and releasing layer after layer of strategies and coping mechanisms can feel scary to the inner child. For so long you have developed these strategies to protect yourself from being hurt and now you are asked to let them go.

Why should I let them go, you may ask*? Don't these strategies fulfill a purpose?*

Yes, indeed, we say, as we hug you, surrounding you with a melody and scents that may be heard and perceived by the ones linked to their pure light. So much of whom you are is lost and buried by these strategies, and, the more you release and shed them, the more your power grows and your luminosity increases. When you stand free and clear of walls, you are vibrating the sound of the "I am," and all who cross your path, are affected.

Vulnerability comes as you make peace with your divinity, letting go of all the costumes you have designed. You stand tall and you feel. When your heart opens to the child hiding inside of you, you may feel like you are having a heart attack. The panic of the heart being exposed may feel like you can no longer stand on your feet, that you may break into a cold sweat, with tears rolling down your face. This child wants to come out from hiding. It wants to play again, and it surely wishes to laugh again. A child sees darkness where it is unable to make anything out. For a child, darkness is dangerous and many wish to sleep with the light on. As you re-connect with that child, the fear ingrained in the imagination of that youngster may visit you again, emerging from the deep cavern of the mind where fear is usually hiding. You will need to face these fears. They are nothing more than large soap bubbles, which are asking to be poked. Nowhere in your multi-dimensional manuals does it ask you to act mature, and nowhere are you being asked to take this journey seriously. You are told over and over again that you are loved regardless of your choices, as love is your birthright. You are also being reminded that you are a master, an angel in human clothes, and, at any given moment, you may choose light over dark. A child's purity is a phase from which all must graduate. In fact, if a child acts too childishly, they are being sent to special schools and tagged by your society as slow or immature. You praise maturity, condemning childish behaviors early on. On the path of light, it is the pure version of you that is carrying the most light. When you come full circle, we ask you to again re-introduce yourself to the child in you and bring it back to light. She has been hiding for too long. You are beautiful in every way. At times you only feel close to being a child when you are about to end your cycle and no longer have the physical capacity to take care of self. Only then, you may get glimpses of what once was you. Each moment that you allow yourself to be the child all over again is a gift.

How do we begin to make contact with that child you ask?

It is simple, you clear your schedule for a period of time and you plan nothing. You walk about or lie down and just be. Observe and witness your surroundings. Even for a short while, let your mind wander and the wonder will begin to bubble. All you need to do in the beginning is take the time, allowing the child to re-emerge. Your mind always wishes to think and often finds reasons for worry. It is your old programming, so, when you take time for yourself, teach yourself to play all over again.

You are a pure light, and you descend for a short while to experience expressing through the physical. You come with so much joy and reverence into a human body, knowing fully what you are about to face, as you flow through the terrain of your journey. The heavy dense reality on this planet is challenging for a subtle energy like you, so you build shields to ease the sensations, pains, and hurts that you absorb from your environment.

As you shield yourself from pain, you also shield yourself from feeling and connecting to the pure source within you. You spend much of your developmental phase building barriers and strategies to shield self from the heavy energies, protecting the pure child residing inside. A child's laughter sounds like nothing else in the universe. It heals. It is a weightless carrier of joy an adult can rarely experience.

When you watch your child laugh, become still, offering gratitude for the opportunity to be a witness to divinity in action. Know that you are a child and you always will be, that age is but an illusion you may only discover, at times, when it is too late.

There are many of you who are experiencing challenges, seemingly one after the other, as this is the time we spoke of and it is here, beautiful in all its complexity and poignancy. Heaviness, beliefs, appropriateness, old programming, all are being challenged now. Much of what you believe is "you" does not truly belong to you, and many are recognizing this and it feels terrible.

Many feel as if they have been misled and they are only now discovering that the structure they built their life on was made out of nothing more than a deck of cards. Many are terrified of being lighter, of shedding weight, of freeing themselves from anchors. You are fighting to remain heavy for dear life because you do not know any other way. The structures you were led to believe that you couldn't survive without are crumbling. Let go, we ask you with a smile. The easier you let go, the simpler will be your flight into laughter and light. Be ready to let go of the old and do not replace what you know with something else you know. Let new replace the old. Open the door and play, what serves you will meander to you. It is a law that, when you revel in joy, joy comes to you, and when you lay with fear; scary sights will cross your path. Open the sanctuary of your heart, allowing light to pierce the closet and break the lock to the door under which you locked away your inner child.

It is time to be fearless and it is time to search for that child again. And so be it.

The Test

Yes, you may wish to cry, but now is not the time. It is time to be in the energy of the truth. Then, be detached from what is and remain in your heart. Your conviction must be tested. It is the way of it. The one being tested is sacred, as is the tester. All work within the same arena playing their role. No winners or losers, only players.

Why does it feel so ugly and heavy, you ask in disbelief?

Because this is Earth when it chooses darkness. It is on you now to practice what you know and move above what you see, connecting to light all the time. Illuminate and be still. Darkness never holds power over light—ever. Only when light chooses to play by the same rules as the dark does it become darker. Remain with light and you will illuminate this planet. This is the choice that is facing you. It faces anyone who has ever walked the highest path on Earth. This is your mettle. You have crossed a threshold of vibration, a sphere of ripple, so now you are being tested.

Any light that has reached a critical mass of souls will be assaulted by the winds of resistance and discredited. You have tried to avoid the resistance, yet there is no avoiding, only facing. Light is not being offered medals on Earth at this time. Light initiates, reveals, and is a catalyst for change. Many of you resist change and would rather close your eyes, blaming the light, than remove the covers from your eyes to face yourselves. Facing self and loving self is, and always will be, your greatest challenge. Many of you go to extreme lengths to avoid seeing the real you, telling yourself stories. One moment you are loved and the next moment you are despised by the same elements. Within cosmic law, these two movements are one and the same. One feels wonderful; the other feels painful. Your role is to be balanced with both; not moved by adorations and not swayed by admonitions. Remain in your core, knowing that all is in order, that the movement is just a movement, with one side always swaying over to the other in due time.

Why have I experienced that which I am experiencing, you ask?

We smile as we hug you once again. We remind you that we have heard this question more than a few times before and we wish you to know that all is guided in cosmic order. You are facing a choice, at any given moment, how to be, rather than to become. Hold on to your light and detach from the movement. Allow it to move through you and observe. Watch the pain of Earth and the delight of Earth. Attach to neither. To hold the balance you must first be tested to find balance within you. You are being cleansed, cleared, and prepped for your role. Find a way to connect to your heart and offer gratitude for the initiations that are presented to you. Learn from each breath, each movement, each feeling, and each thought while attaching to none. Observe those around you moving with the drama. Observe their choices, their convictions, and their beliefs. Watch them and shine. Allow them to despise you and allow them to love you without floating from your center. Maintain your equilibrium and connect to your core light. This is your reality. Your love of self is being tested and your core truth is being pushed to its limits. Hold on to nothing and move with the wind. Do not resist the pain, and do not resist the agony. Move deeper into yourself and you will find that in the deepest cavern of your heart there is only light and it shines so bright that it forgives and holds compassion for each human regardless of their choices. You are asked to love your detractors. You are asked to have compassion for those who choose to use the language of light as a weapon. Each one of you, each moment, is being given a choice to be in your truth, to be in your light, to be in oneness, to respect each human as an extension of the other, or, to be in duality and fear, to close the light and let the power of love hide in the closet, locked away. This is your choice at this time and there is no sitting this one out.

If you are the one who wishes to discover what you are made of, you must choose. Whether you choose light or dark, the universe presents to you the result of your choices. It is an impersonal law named karma. All movements include karmic processes and are being accelerated on Earth, and the sum choices of an angel are coming due today for debt taken on yesterday. There is no longer a delay of lifetime's separate cause and effect. Those who violate cosmic laws and know better must pay for these violations within the same lifetime. You wanted to graduate and this is what it takes. We are with you at every moment and you are never ever alone. No matter what you perceive as a hostile environment, facing immense challenges, the light is always with you. Connect to it and know that all is in order. There are no mistakes, no punishments, and no victims, only choices upon choices reflected and projected, back to you, on the silver screen you call "real life".

There is no duality when you reside in your heart. You and your detractors are one, you and your lover are one, you and the elements are one, and you and the planet are one. You must understand that cancer is one's own cells mutating and attacking themselves. These cells go against the idea of oneness, eventually dismissing the entire body, so that in fact, both the cancer cells as well as the healthy cells die since they are really both aspects of one singular body. The same applies for those who attack, those who cause harm, those who steal, and kill, using their power rather than their hearts. They are like cancer eating at the self. Any cell can turn cancerous. It is by choice. You are all aspects of the one, the same way darkness and light are both aspects of the one, good and bad, high and low are one, heavy and light, big and small, all polarity is a movement within a container that is always one. You can never eradicate dark because it is just a lack of light, but you can shine all the time, then the darkness will not be expressed. Darkness is always a potential that becomes form when one turns off their light. You are all aspects of all that is, and together you are God expressed in physical form. The movement all around you is an initiation for each one to choose, to examine, core beliefs; to go deep within and explore what it means to be a human angel. Some of you believe that you came to save someone else, but in all truth all you need to be is you in an awakened state, shining and radiating love to all. When you do reside in your heart you benefit all. The reason for the ever-growing frequency and intensity of storms, internally and externally, is to rearrange what was and re-create a potential for a new physical reality simultaneously removing blockages and changing paradigms. Your planetary reality is shifting now moment by moment. Many are being assaulted and barraged with life changing movement that is constant, leaving you with little safety and even less security. This is the way of it. You are asked to trust. If you truly hold the core belief that all is in divine order, you also know that the changes that are now facing you are here to support you on your journey higher. You are an initiator and a catalyst for others. You came to Earth to create movement and guide those who seek to find the light. You guide by being in your heart, by being in the place of love and balance.

What am I supposed to do, you ask?

Know that all is in order and no aspect of the one is ever lacking. Know that all movements in essence are guided by cosmic energy, which sways from one polarity to the other creating cycles, and you are asked to navigate within these cycles. Your ancient cultures knew of the cycles and were guided by the cosmic movement they observed.

You are one with all that is and you carry within you at any moment the full spectrum of light, dark, and shades of gray. Each moment and each breath are a test. Whenever you move one way, know that a counter-movement will surely come, so stay as balanced as you can. Breathe deeply and be in gratitude. Keep your heart open. Radiate love to all, compassion to all, because you are all. When you do, you begin to understand what self-love means. It does not mean that you love only self. It means that you see all as a reflection of the self and when you have love and compassion for self it is extended to all that is. We are now holding you dear and letting you know that you are loved and that you are never alone. You are asked to spread your multi-dimensional wings and fly above the drama, above the pain, above the storyline, and see all as just a movement. Let this movement rage and let the elements rearrange all that you know to be, while holding on to your truth. We are asking you to be what you came here to be, an angel in human form. And so be it.

The Rainbow

You ask that I sit in front of you on the same chair that I introduced myself to you and held your hand, but the chair is empty and there is no one except you.

Yes, I do not see anyone. Why did everyone disappear? You inquire.

We are all here with you, and in fact we are all around you. You do not see us this time but if you let your heart open you will feel us. We know who you are; it is not us for whom you are searching. You are searching for your truth and you are searching for your light. Your truth is sitting on the empty chair.

But it is empty, we hear you think to yourself.

Indeed it is, we smile, and it is time for you to fill that chair and sit in it.

But I am already sitting across from it, you reply frustrated.

With a hug we ask you to get up and move to the empty chair. In quantum reality, or in our reality, you will then be sitting in both chairs simultaneously, as time is not linear. We ask you to take a leap of faith, fully accepting that you are a multidimensional being existing on more than one playing field at a time. You are asked to be flying and walking, bridging dimensions, experiencing, when appropriate, being in a place of darkness as well as in a place of light, knowing from your core that you cannot be described only in terms of light or dark, as you are an aspect of God and your role is to be a conduit for love, a vessel for change, and a catalyst for accelerated movement around you. You are a vessel and those who are touched by your field translate their own shifting internally; painting their own canvas; choosing the various shades of gray based on their own awareness and vantage point. As we hug you, we say: Never attach to the drama swirling around you, never attach to love or adoration projected at you, and never identify with how others paint you. You will be called light, you will be called dark, you will be named names. Know that you are just a mirror, a phantom, a projection for others to see themselves. When you are tagged as dark, you are reflecting the darkness of the one sitting across from you. When you are called light, you reflect the light to the one sitting across from you. You are all and you are none. We ask you to walk empty and free. You are being liberated and released from being "good." You are freed from being "bad." You are being freed from expectations and demands; you are being freed from gravity so you can exist in the purest form of the "I am." Being "good" is a trap, being "bad" is a trap, being free is being neither. Being free is embracing the totality of existence within the spectrum of the rainbow, creating a circle that is a reflection of light, where each hue represents the angle of the light hitting the raindrops. None of it is "you" and all of it is "you." It is time for you to be free from holding on to how others perceive you. Clear your attachments, sever the cords, break the chains, and move away from the human angel's ambivalent duality-based consciousness, acknowledging that once you have crossed the threshold, there is no going back. Do not look back, embrace your fragile frame and keep walking as you are being initiated to withstand zero gravity, yet remain connected to all planes, heaven or Earth. You are being initiated to a higher peak and the air is thin; the vista is breathtaking but each breath takes some getting used to. Slow down, as each step you take leads you higher and higher in the never-ending journey towards reuniting with your God-self.

Breathe and feel the pulse of the universe as it moves through you. Trust in the perfection of the movement of the stars, moon, and sun. All movements are predictable and precisely guided by the forces at play. When you are familiar with those forces, you know the "why" as well as the "how" of each movement. You encounter no surprises following celestial bodies in motion, because you know their paths, when they rise and when they set, and you know how their gravitational fields affect each other as you have been observing them for eons studying their trajectories. It is the same with your human roadmap on the physical plan. The cosmic law "as above, so below" always applies and is always precise. All elements and forces expressed in the cosmic playing fields determine the celestial movement, adhering to predictable laws. When a celestial body wobbles or goes off its expected path, you infer that some unseen gravitational forces have played a role. Know that indeed the movement that affects your current physical reality is always an accurate expression of the various universal forces interacting with your angelic frequency. Whenever an acceleration of your journey is intended, you are being dislodged from the comfort of your sanctuary and tossed along a new route. This movement may not feel comfortable or safe, nevertheless, we ask you to trust that no movement is arbitrary and all is of your choosing, by your consent.

I do not recall agreeing to this, you protest.

We can assure you that all is by agreement and that your memory will come back to you one day not too far into your future. It happens in everyone's life all the time. On your personal path, you face shifts that may feel, at times, organic and harmonious in nature, while, at other times, sharp and violent. There is no difference, from spirit's perspective, how you get to where you need to go or how you learn a lesson. Your light chooses from the infinite possibilities, floating in your potential future the one which serves you, and all those around you, the most.

No, you say, *I would have never chosen to inflict pain on myself.*

With a smile we say to you, yes you did. It is because the choice you make comes from your expanded self, which does not judge pain or suffering as bad, and joy or happiness as good. It is guided by the rule that you came here to serve the larger self—which is an aspect of God—and therefore, whatever serves the larger you is being chosen. One can always choose not to grow, but you only postpone the inevitable, which is not in line with your purpose. Your purpose is to grow and reunite with that larger you, that aspect of God. As you move through the different developmental stages, you collect experiences, which in turn become your treasure, trophies the soul collects throughout lifetimes of being in physical form.

What is it that you are trying to tell me, you ask?

We are trying to tell you to relax and allow the movement being expressed all around you to fulfill its agreements with all the gravitational forces playing their role, not trying to impose your will, as it would only divert the intended trajectory and cause delays. Everything in the universe has its own unique rhythm, its own unique vibration, and its own unique direction. Each time you are in a place of love and your heart is pulsing the kind of rhythm that supports the universal melody, you are allowing that which is God to play a role on Earth. When you are not in that vibration, you create a disconnect which sounds like a musical instrument that is out of tune. There are many who play in this symphony and each musical instrument adds its own unique vibration. You are not to judge the drums as more effective or positive than the trumpets or violins. All has its place. Your place is to be in sync with the melody and be part of the symphony.

There are a few who come to Earth to facilitate the shifting of a melody and redirect the players from "pop" to "jazz" in alignment with the Earth's cosmically planned trajectory, but in the end all music is honored whether it is this or that. Some wished that they could silence their own sound but you cannot. It is why you are here. Your choice is limited to how you play. You can try to hide under a rock, but wherever you may be hiding, your melody is still heard. Your choices are not whether to be part of the orchestra or not, but whether you play awakened or asleep. The largest majority of Earth's humans are sleeping. Most do not correlate their lives with the physical reality manifesting in their world and they crown their governments, politics, conspiracies or God, luck, and a slew of other powers for creating the particular circumstances in which they find themselves. Few assume full responsibility over their physical reality and you are one of them. We ask you to own up to each tone being played and offer gratitude. Your melody will then create light in harmony with the universal symphony being played.

To create a change in your physical reality you must follow two steps: align fully with your current reality taking full responsibility for what is, then offer gratitude for where you are presently, and the role you were meant to play. These two profound steps open the gate for you to change your reality almost instantaneously. You are a vibration, and when your resonance is aligned with love, you affect all. It would seem unfathomable to some if we would say that positive and negative experience in a lifetime is really neither. A journey in each cycle begins with circumstance seemingly out of your control. The more awakened you are, the more you realize that all is in your control and the movement within your cycle is always neutral. Your reaction is the only dark and light in this equation of your Earth cycle. No one, no matter how horrific the circumstances may seem to you, is being forgotten by God or somehow left on the sidelines. Your Earth cycle is always a role and never the real you. It is just a small portion of your vast story being expressed in this physical dimension. Some come here for a short cycle and some for longer, but within the vast time-space continuum, the celestial tapestry, your movement lasts as long as a shooting star, so it is no wonder that so many wish to be stars during this short expression (angelic humor). Some hold on to the belief that without making an impact, what is the sense of such a brief visit? With a smile, we ask you to look at yourself in the mirror and allow your face to become transparent until such a time that you connect to your true light and no longer attach to a personality. When you pierce the veil you become everything and everything becomes you. Only when you dissolve your self, can you begin to feel the vastness of your energy and the impact you have on your universe. You are eternal and you exist in a paradox of sorts. You are nothing and everything simultaneously; you have no choice, yet everything is your choice; you never die, but you also never really live; you are permanent, yet fleeting; you affect all, while mostly believing that you have very little effect over your own life, let alone the lives of others. The way you perceive your life is a direct expression of your vibration. The vantage point of your awareness determines how much credit you give yourself for creating all that you encounter in your physical dimension. When asleep, you are less able to connect the dots and see how you are being served by all that is happening to you. Being awakened or asleep you are loved the same and, from our perch, there is never a judgment or hierarchy as to your placement along the spiritual continuum. Moreover, it does not make a difference if you are aware of the cosmic laws which guide your life or not, the laws apply just the same. When you begin to take responsibility over all that is being expressed in your life, you have turned on your light which grows brighter as you learn to love the true self and offer gratitude for who you are. The game of life is played within a magnificent and mysterious puzzle. The most sacred aspect of playing the game is simply taking part in it, being in a physical body. Solving the puzzle is not the goal, playing is the goal. Solving the puzzle is a by-product. You may face a specific riddle, which may not be solved this lifetime, or even the next, but eventually you do figure a way to resolve it. There is a celebration, and you promptly move to the next puzzle advancing ever forward. An old soul you are, and as you awaken you realize that cosmic laws operate in a consistent and predictable way. Being in harmony with those laws is how you advance. With a smile we say, it is time to crack these codes.

There is a vast spiraling energy that is coming your way and it shifts all particles on its path, like a cosmic "tornado." Your collective fuels the power of this swirling energy and the quality of it is determined by your state of grace. This tornado will be moving through the Earth plane within the next thirteen months and your role is to be prepared by being in harmony with self, feeling love, and being in tune with your own melody. Those of you who are not anchored within their own playing field may be tossed in the air by these powerful cosmic forces, which are immense. This tornado cannot be described in terms of positive or negative. It can be described as challenging and intense; one that may accelerate and shift the lives of many. Some of you are asked to hold the bridge for others so get ready, move into your power, and become free.

The swirling vortex is but one of the waves meant to create a mass movement within your accelerated path. The few must maintain equanimity for the many.

W*hy is it thirteen months and why are you telling us now?* You ask.

We tell you because this is the reason you came here, to be a beacon, a lighthouse, a shield of love that connects all. Understand that cosmic movements, which begin at the edge of time, create portals of energy from which events are being stirred and directed long before they actually can be seen or physically felt.

What is it that we should do? How should we prepare? You ask.

Be in joy is our answer, be in gratitude, celebrate each day as it comes, slow down, and welcome whatever is to cross your path with full trust. Be in your heart and love all that you see without judging it. Offer gratitude and understand that the only control you can exercise when in the midst of the swirling vortex is your reaction. Become disciplined and you will not only reward yourself but all. Nowhere and at no time, was physical reality on Earth so closely monitored by your galactic neighbors. At no time in your history as human angels, was your spiritual awakening so directly linked to the physical manifestation of matter. You are now aligning with your core purpose here and yet too few are awakened to this fact that each thought, each intention, and each action is measured on a scale either on the side of light or darkness. We wish you always to choose light, be light; allow those who reside in darkness to dwell where they may be and shine. Embrace light through love and allow those in darkness the choice to transform. You are at the edge of the swirling movement that may feel very uncomfortable to many. It is indeed appropriate and on schedule. Allow that which may come to pass by knowing full well that you are where you need to be and meant to be playing your role. Do reside in the sanctuary of gratitude; reside in the sanctuary of your heart; reside in a place of love and rejoice for the sacred play unfolding in your theater called Earth, and so be it.

Two Become One

Love is all you have to consider. There is no other consideration. Wherever you are, you are but a flowing stream of consciousness interacting with your surroundings. Your experiences are not external but always internal. Therefore the lens you put on as you are streaming determines the colors you perceive.

I already knew that, you say.

You are in the land of the angels. There are many of us here in human form facilitating Earth. Do you feel us?

I do not feel you, in particular, but I feel that my heart is open and I sense love all around, you say.

Then you do feel us. Not even a feather can be airborne without some type of energy to push it higher. You all require energy; it is what keeps you alive. When it is time to let the body die, your energy is retracted from the body and leaves. This energy fills your being right before birth and it leaves the body right before what you call death. This energy does not have a beginning nor does it ever end, but it manifests in various forms. When it enters you, it does not signal the birth of the energy because the energy always was. It only means the birth of this particular energy merging with a particular form. When this energy chooses to retract, it does not signify the death of the energy but only the end of the marriage between this particular energy with this particular form. The form dies but the energy is eternal.

Why are you telling us things we already know? You ask.

There are many things you claim to know but that you need to be reminded about again, and yet again, at different junctures on your journey. When you come with another angel into a sacred union, until "death do you part" as your sacred matrimonial ceremony reads, it does not mean that one of the two must die if you separate, it only means that the energy that fueled this sacred union has retracted and therefore can no longer holds the union together. Indeed it may feel like death, and allegorically it is called a death, but no one necessarily really dies. Your contract reads that you change and transform continuously. You change shapes, forms, costumes, and circumstances, but your energy lives on, as an aspect of the great "I am," changing colors and melody but eternally connected to source and true to its purpose.

The purpose of two angel beings coming together is for creation. One human angel form merging with another human angel form creates a unique "story" that is unlike the two when they are separated. There is always a purpose of two coming together, the timing of a beginning and the timing of an ending are as sacred as any birth and death. When two become one they, in fact, become three. Long before you have created a child through birth you have created a third being that is the two forms merged. You come into unions as a creative act, and each time you merge you have created a new form. This form can be described as a ripple of energy that carries a unique frequency blend of the two combined, broadcasting the energetic union. This unique energy will keep on "living" whether it ever expresses itself through matter or not. It will search for a form to come into expression but it does not require this form to remain "alive." This new form of energy is not really "new" and was not manifested through birth, as it always existed, but its unique flavor, color, and melody was created through the merger of two angelic beings. It is why we ask you to merge through love and not through anything else such as anger or revenge. Merging through love creates a ripple of energy that is in search of an expression that resonates with the vibration in which it was created. This ripple can also be described as a being. Beings who were created not through love will seek, likewise, an expression similar in tonal resonance to the vibration, which created them. When the two become one through love they create a being of love, and when they do not, they may manifest a being of darkness. This is how it works.

You are an aspect of God and as such, unknowingly or knowingly, you create energetically through merging. Cultures of the past and cultures which exist in your time, when in cycles of darkness, expand their circle of influence controlling and limiting the frequencies which are at the core of this sacred union.

Why are you sharing this now? You ask.

Be aware of what you create and, to safeguard your creation, be in a place of love. It is your purpose, it is your power, it is your legacy, it is your child, and it is your light. Imagine that you are an angel with wings, flying over Earth sprinkling it with specks of golden dust. This dust settles on the earth and penetrates the soil; it absorbs moisture and soaks in the sun. At one point it transforms itself, as if through magic, into a seed, which in turns begins to grow. This seed gives form to a tree. The tree grows more seeds which are being carried away by the winds, the bees, and the animals. These seeds spread everywhere, being deposited in the soil, to be awakened at some point by water and light, becoming form. This is your legacy, to spread the golden dust which will be inserted, as if by magic, to the game of creation and, when the time is right, will grow and morph into a form. You are on a journey and confusing this journey is, we say with a wink. It is confusing because the knowing is not linear, the path never straight, the blocks and tests are ample, and growing more challenging.

Why is this so, you ask?

No one ever said that this journey is a walk in the park. It is so because this game has much riding on it. Each and every curve offers opportunities to examine, re-examine, clear, and move through the debris that accumulated over millennia. It is why you are here. You did not choose this ride based on ease or comfort.

Why did I choose it? You ask.

You came here this time around because you knew you could make a difference in the lives of many. Many of you old souls chose to be here at this time, being in harm's way, at times, so you could help transform what was dark into light. Many of you could have remained in energy form helping from beyond the veil, but you also knew that there is an opportunity for a shift and your service was needed. Many of you volunteered to come and hold space for others who are now awakening. We wish you to honor yourself and your service knowing that it is "now" the time you were seeing in the viewing chambers. The dice are rolled each time there is a shift in energy and the shifts are now more intense and more frequent than ever before. You are required to be more precise than ever, more disciplined than ever, more trusting than ever, and more in your heart than ever before. You are asked to move forward and not to look back, you are asked to be prescient, awakened, sharp, clear, perceptive, and discerning. Listen to the subtle signs and sounds, letting them lead you forward. Follow your inner guidance and know that this is your highest authority. Learn to distinguish between what comes from within and what comes from the outside. Great noise is now in the ethers and those who are not clear may pick up chatter, which they may mistake for their own, and follow it. Learn to be in silence, know what is yours and what is not.

There is a great shift that is on the way and your work has to be prepared. The bells will be ringing in many of the energy centers on Earth and sparks will be flying where codes have been active and awake. The streams that you and your fellow angels are facilitating may be merging with other streams, creating a larger river, more potent than any individual stream. Watch for signs and watch the sky. The signs come from seemingly everywhere, but will appear clearly in the night's sky. Do not be concerned with logistics, be in your heart. All else is part of the stream which leads to the ocean. Trust that it is so.

You speak in riddles, you say. *Can you guide us more clearly?* You ask.

We do, but not through writing. Like in any computer program, it is not sufficient to write the content; there must be context, which is in place to translate the code into a legible result. We are now offering the software so that, when the time is right, you can decipher the language of signs.

The words in the messages are always energetic, first, allowing the one reading the language of angels to use its software to translate signs, so truth can be distinguished from falsehood.

It is always a choice to be in light or to be in darkness. Those of you who have read our words, yet chose darkness, did so fully aware. Those of you who read our words and chose light did so fully aware. We are messengers of light, but the choice of what to do with your own energy, once you are awakened, is yours and yours alone. We can hug you, love you, guide you, embrace you, and show you the high road, but the choice of where to tread is yours and yours only.

The mystery of mysteries is that you are the one who chooses and creates your own path, while we are your entourage facilitating, when allowed, and loving always.

It is with tears of joy that we are dancing with you each time, and it is with immense honor that we are saying thank you for allowing us to reach out and hug you. You are asked to be in your truth, awakened, and allow others to find the light through your light. We wish you to safeguard your light always, and so be it.

The Cell

You are dearly loved.

I have heard that before but I do not feel loved at the moment.

Feeling loved is one thing but being loved is yet another.

What do you mean? You wonder.

When you walk the street of New York, you may feel that you are separated from all the people who walk by you. They are dressed differently than you, speaking languages you do not understand, and seem to be preoccupied with their own business, paying no attention to you or to anyone outside their immediate circle. As they walk and talk, act and interact, they appear to be separated, individuated, by appearance and language, yet, they are not.

How do you reconcile being one and many simultaneously? How do you reconcile being loved and hated simultaneously? How do you reconcile being part of all that is yet maintaining the appearance of an individual walking the street of New York City, minding your own business? You are like an individual cell in a body. To the cell (you) it feels as if it is by itself, fending for its survival, moving about, interacting and exchanging with other cells, being attacked at times, by "white" cells and defended by "red" cells. The reality of the cell is one of difficult struggles, at times, as it is being born, grows, and dies. It experiences hunger deprivation, and, at times, joy and abundance. The cell, from its perspective, is like you from your perspective. The cell cannot envision the whole body as one. It cannot really experience the working of all the cells towards a mutual goal. It cannot move out of the body. It can only "see" the friends, relatives, and associate cells moving about, with each one having its own responsibility and role. An individual cell, though, does not have the capacity to see itself as part of a whole. Yet, it plays its role perfectly, digesting, attacking, defending, absorbing, oozing, and communicating. That cell is you and that body is all of you: humanity, your galactic family, the cosmos. The further you venture, the larger the body becomes.

The cell that "works" in the liver department may raise its awareness to see all its associates in the liver department as family, friends, and co-workers. As it ventures higher and higher in awareness, it may experience the whole body as one; later, all the other bodies as part of the same system, and, eventually, all that is. You and the person across the street, who is dressed differently, speaks a different language, and walks the opposite direction, are part of the same body of cells working and existing in the same system, towards the same goal. And when you venture high enough, you see all of the cells as representing one body: you.

When enough cells work in unison towards the same goal, they create a coherent message to the body that it is loved, that it is needed, and that its growth and health are supported. The essence of each cell in your body is love, as well as light. The essence of each human walking their path on Earth is love and light. The cell is conscious in the same way that the human is conscious. Indeed there are levels of awareness, but each cell has an awareness of self and its environment. The macro and the micro are always linked, reflecting the same basic truth. We have come thus far to guide you; to fill your path with light so you could venture above your immediate surroundings; to acknowledge who you are. Cells are born and die all the time, but often, other cells are replacing them; at times the whole body dies yet another one is being reborn. All movement is encapsulated within one system many of you name God: a system that is vast, yet, so intimately connected to each and every one of you, whether you acknowledge it or not. You are a miracle who manifested from the cosmos. You are not simply a planet Earth creation. You are a cosmic consciousness residing in a body designed as a vessel to carry the spirit of all. You are part of all and all is part of you. Each of you plays a particular role just the same as different cells play different roles within your body. Yet, in addition, your consciousness represents the entire cosmos. The hidden and the revealed are equal. What you can perceive always will be equal to what is hidden from you.

Why is it so?

As you move higher and see more of the panoramic view surrounding you, you understand how much is yet hidden from you. Knowledge is not your goal, playing your role is the goal. There are billions of cells in your body, with each playing a role. None of your cells are aware of the entire body yet they are all working for it. You, like the cell, work for the entire body, whether you acknowledge it or not. The difference is that you, unlike the cell, have a choice and that choice is the subject of this message.

What is the choice? And why is there a choice? You ask.

Choice creates movement of energy. Movement is an innate aspect of the system of creation. Movement requires energy. Choice is energy. The higher consciousness is, the more it is aware of itself, the more choices it has, and the more energy it produces. You represent consciousness and therefore reside in a free will zone. Your choices are energy creators, which fuel the cosmic movement of growth. There is great interest in your choices because you do not exist in a vacuum. You are connected to all that is and the galactic family is aware of the entire body as well as of your role within this body. As you make choices, you direct the movement of the cosmic waves rippling from planet Earth outward. These seemingly weak waves of energy never stop expanding. They continue to expand through space, affecting movements of particles on the other side of the Milky Way. Some of you believe that you are small and helpless, but you are not. Like a cell, you reside in a magnificent body and you are responsible for its well-being because you are a part of it. A choice is the result of awareness, a movement, a desire, an energy, which is an aspect of consciousness.

Who is the one choosing? You may ask. *Well, is it me?* You say.

With a smile we ask yet again, who is you? Is it the liver, the heart, the foot, the cell? Who?

You say, *it is my thinking brain.*

Then, we ask, is it the gray matter in your skull that makes the choices? Is it the neurons, cells, molecules, or the atoms, which make up the gray matter that makes a choice?

We hear you say in frustration, *why does it matter?*

We hug you now and say, because this is how loved you are. All layers of your being participate on some level in your choices. From the great "I am" to the atoms which form molecules which make up the building blocks of your cells. From the macro to the micro, all aspects of "you" partake in the process of making choices and each choice affects the entire body. Now you can understand why you matter. You, like the cell, participate in the decision making of the whole body continuously. Each thought, feeling, action, reaction, or movement may create a change for the entire collective body. You are so loved. Although prevented from making the obvious link between what is in front of you and you, yet you are determined to search for answers. You are so loved, because you need to be reminded what you already know: that you are made out of love; that you matter; that you are here to create a change within you and have that change affect all. Now you may understand that, like the one cell, which affects the whole, so you too, can change the whole collective system of which you are a part.

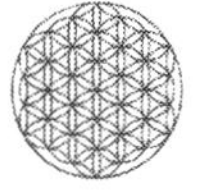

If we are one, then why is there so much strife and discord? You ask.

This is your work. It is your purpose to become one in all aspects of your being. You are one as energy, and the reason for your coming into the portal of human existence is to create oneness within you, merging and uniting with the great "I am." You are born as one and you die as one. The whole middle section of your journey is your work, your purpose. You came here to grow and learn by making choices on your path without having clear signposts. You come to re-learn and reestablish your connection with the great "I am."

Why do I come to suffer, when the alternative is so appealing being in a place of peace and unity, you wonder?

This is not exactly so, we say with a smile. When you are in a place of peace and unity, all that you wish for is to come back to the Earth plane so that you may fight, learn, grow, develop, expand, create, and love. You wish, with all your angelic being, to experience Earth life because it is so exciting, so mysterious, so challenging, and so sacred. As an energy, many of the experiences are not available to you, the visceral, emotional sensation of being in love, of pain, of joy. These are very different when you are in a pure energy form.

How so, you ask?

When you are in spirit, as pure energy, you have no mass, and you do not really experience yourself as separated from all that is. You are a drop in the ocean that is both aware of itself as a drop, yet aware of the ocean. The movements of the ocean are the movement of the drop and the movement of the drop is the same as the movement of the ocean. They are both separated and the same, an oxymoron where two seemingly contradictory statements represent truth. As pure energy you are in a state of being, in a state of harmony, in a state of peace. You have work, much of it, but the work does not feel like work. It is a mere playing your role, like a cell playing its role. If you think that, by being a pure energy you rest, the answer is no. You never really rest. You are busy at the work of creation, both in form and in energy, yet that experience of both is very different and all of you yearn to be in physical form so you can test yourself, grow, create, be challenged, and move forward on your path to reunite with self. You come to experience a free will that is not available, in the same form, when you are energy. Choice is a privilege that you all wish to experience. When you are in a state of peace, all you wish for is action. When you are here on planet Earth, experiencing action, many of you do wish to be back with us experiencing only peace. Being connected to both heaven and Earth, finding balance, while becoming a pure vessel for love, and manifesting a bridge of light into form, this is your challenge. Your task is to merge both dimensions so you become peaceful with what is, and ripple that peace to everyone who comes in contact with you. Your mission, taking a human form, is as sacred as it gets. If we had told you of the lines, queuing in the waiting area, for angels to emerge in form you would be astounded. The horrors and challenges you experience, at times, as a human, feel very different when you are watching it from the other side of the veil. Your essence is of love; you are born to form so that you may exercise choice. Your choices affect all and that is the purpose. You experience separation so you may learn about unity; you experience fear so you can learn about trust; you experience hate so that you could learn about love. You experience pain to learn about pleasure. You are a form that learns about its self from all angles. The physical dimension is a dream, which was designed to feel real. Although all your experiences are internal, your biology is wired to sense your experiences as if they are external.

Why? You wonder.

If you were "convinced" that it is all a "joke," an illusion, and that you can never truly be harmed, why would you desire to learn to fly? If you have nothing to lose, why would you work so hard? You will ignore the alarm clock and never get out of bed. This movie has to be real, with real consequences, real emotions, real pain, and real stakes. Only when you are out of the game can you see the beauty and perfection of it, the illusion of it, and, yes, the humor if it as well. You can then evaluate where you were and how best to continue the work where you left off. If you knew that you are invincible, you just would not try as hard. This is why the stakes are high and your choices do make a difference, because this movie in this dimension is real to you. Only when you find yourself out of this dimension does the storyboard change. You are a cell, part of a divine body and you are working with the entire system to create, to expand, to grow while remaining balanced. Choice is your greatest gift in this physical dimension; a choice to exist in unity consciousness or not. When you do choose to see your self as a part of all that is, your storyboard is aligning, when you perceive your self as separated, you are asleep, your storyboard is often misaligned.

When you understand your power, your divinity, your role, and you acknowledge the possibility that each breath, thought, action, and reaction is affecting all that is, you turn on your light, which guides all. This is your mission and why you are here at this time, and so be it.

The Divine Plan

You are dearly loved.

All movement takes place in circles. Many of you believe that you are moving forward, although, in fact, you are spinning all around the core energy of your lesson. As you ascend, obstacles that appeared large and daunting become small specks of dust on your windshield so that you now hardly notice. Your journey is about movement, change, growth, expansion, and yes, ascension. You are always within reach of your learning. Each moment, each breath, each heartbeat is a new promise to grow, open, expand, allow, enable, flow, and surrender, awakening to the true magnificence of your being.

There is an immense beauty emanating from those of you who have conquered fear and are walking in harmony with the knowledge that all is part of a divine plan and nothing is arbitrary. If you knew truly and completely that you are loved, cared for, protected, and guided, would you still have a reason to worry, be scared, be a victim? If you knew that you can never fail on this journey, and that all lessons end up serving the divine plan, regardless of whether its intent came from dark or light, would you still doubt that you are where you need to be? If, every day, you would receive a note detailing the amazing feats you can accomplish today, all the potentials of new beginnings that each breath offers, would you still have an excuse to feel defeated? Each day, each breath, and each heartbeat are a world unto itself, opening the gate for you to awaken to a new state of grace; a world of beauty, where love reigns and darkness is banished. The molecules of oxygen entering your lungs and the photons of light hitting your corneas carry within them the potential to transmute what was, a minute ago, darkness, into the sun's brilliance. This is your story, one of glory, regardless of whether you are aware of it or not, regardless of you ever awakening to your truth, still, it is a story of glory. Have you ever considered the possibility that whatever you encounter as an obstacle, a painful challenge, is the way you teach yourself the art of flying? No sailboat can reach its destination without headwinds. No bird can fly without the resistance of air and the pull of gravity. You are an actor and you learn to play your role the best that you can. An aspect of your role is to interact with your fellow actors, along with your audience, creating a motion and emotions in them, guiding them into awakening and realizing who they are, as well as all the potential they carry to blossom. Your role is and always was to play yourself, being true to your own calling, your own desires, your own proclivities, and your own passion. You often believe that others are your role models so that you must follow their footsteps to reach your destination. With a hug, we offer to you, once more, the possibility that your gift is your uniqueness, your power lies in your truth, in your beauty, and in you playing your own role as best you can. At times, many cycles pass where you walk in the groove set up for you by your ancestors. Sacred it is, but yet, at some point on your eternal journey towards growth, you are presented with the opportunity of awakening and by doing so, most likely walking straight into a headwind, facing a resistance, being beaten down, often ridiculed. And this, dear human, is your moment of glory. These cycles are the cycles you have been waiting for to break molds, remove obstacles, open new fronts, new understandings, pushing against your own limits and those of others, to become airborne, spreading your wings, playing the most sacred role you were destined for, yourself. Where we come from, there are no limits. You have the potential to change everything and anything at the given moment you determine to do so. There is nothing more powerful than the power of your will and intention, so that, when you direct it to move higher, to shine, to be of service, to remove self-limitations and progress through them, you just do it. Many have done so, though many more do not.

You may wonder, *if this is so, why hasn't everyone reached these realizations?*

With a smile, we offer you that, in time, everyone will. It may take another few hundred cycles but still time is not of the essence when you are eternal. That lifetime, that offers the opportunity for so many of you to reach higher, play to your truth, dance to the divine melody of your potential, stretching your boundaries into fields never before explored, that lifetime is now. Many of you know this, yet so few are ready to dance to this new tune.

Why, you ask?

You are carrying so much weight that the pull of gravity discourages many of you from exploring flight. Your story, though, is different from the one told to you by many. You are renegades, emissaries of light, angels in human costumes. You are humans who are gods and goddesses, awakening to the immense potential that each carries, a seed becoming the giant sequoia. You come here to play your role whatever it may be, fully transmuting darkness to light, carrying new frequencies that are more in tune with nature, with the goddess, with Earth, with your heart, and yes, with love. Do you see the sacredness of your coming, the power of your breath and the glory of your heartbeat?

Why, then, cannot everybody see that and dance to the new tune?

Each of you is an aspect of the one; you are all serving that which is the all, each a singular aspect of the "I am." Your individual paths, however, are uniquely different, and they were meant to be so. No two of you are the same, yet all of you are necessary to complete this aspect of creation. Each path offers its own learning, rewards, and challenges. Each of you perceives reality slightly differently. Each lives in a world that is built from its own self-manufactured reality. You do indeed share a reality, but it is only a small portion of who you are and your experience here on Earth. Most of what makes you who you are is created within you, and expressed as a melody, a vibration, a frequency, a picture. Awakening is offered to all of you and it is a potential for more humans now, than since the time of Lemuria, to wear a vibration that is anchored in love, and in tune with Earth. Still, though, within the total inhabitants now occupying your precious plane, it is a comparatively small number.

Why so, you ask?

Most humans are not ready to awaken. They move at their own pace, according to the level of their soul, and the reason they came here. They are as sacred and as powerful as you are, but not ready to acknowledge it nor ready to walk this path. There is nothing wrong with them and they are loved by spirit and guided in the same way as you are, but they are at a different place on this eternal journey and it is appropriate and it is honored.

We hear some of you ask, *how come others cannot see what they are doing to this planet: hurting the young generation, hurting each other? Why can't they just see the futility of it all and just stop?*

With a hug, we tell you that they are just not ready, the same way a two-year-old is unlikely to be ready to take on books and fully understand their content. But they, too, will grow, in time, to see what you see. It does not mean that they are less, they are just at a different place on this journey, and as such, you must find peace with them, as well as understanding. You may feel at times that you are better, but this, my dear angel, is not your truth. All is sacred and it is all an aspect of God. All have a place. We are speaking to you because here it is, your time to truly claim your power, light, your legacy, your truth, and to be a pillar for a bridge now being built. You have worked for centuries to be where you are at present and we are here to remind you that it is "now" the time to remember. You earned your knowing over lifetimes and lifetimes of work. An adult will not brag in front of a two-year-old that she knows better. The adult knows that each age holds its own developmental learning challenges and beauties. The same goes for you. Hold your knowing quiet, wear your vibration without advertising that it is so. Love is quiet, beauty is self-evident, and musical harmony does not need subtitles. You are not asked to convince, preach, or explain to others your truth. You are asked to be your truth, to breathe and ripple love wherever you go. You may not be seen, recognized, or acknowledged. Some may tag you with names and ridicule you. Some may try to block your light; some may even try to cover you with their own blanket so you will not be able to play your role. They will do so in the name of loving you and worrying for you. These may be your close friends, family, lovers, or even your children. Love them and do not hold it against them. They do not know better. Understand that when you live your truth, you shine so brightly that all those who are near you may begin to see using your light. You can never hurt others when you live your truth. Yet, many of you are being accused of being hurtful. Know your truth; know why you are here and what your purpose is. Always act from your heart and you will fulfill the promise you came here to fulfill: being a human angel.

The game of creation is vast; there are many teachers, facilitators and guides to each path. There is not "the one," which fits all. In time all of you must choose a path that is unlike anything anyone ever taught you. It would mean that you find equilibrium sitting in the midst of doubt, fear, worry, and being lost. You find peace in turmoil and you find light in darkness. You find order in disorder, love in hate, harmony in disharmony. You are now a master of your own reality and all that comes to you is transmuted to light, transformed into harmony, order, beauty, and into divinity, where it becomes sacred. Each time one of you is awakened, there is a celebration. Each time human angels come together on a sacred mission to raise the planet's vibration through love, all of us stand ready, in service to you. We are in awe of your power, your commitment, and the strides you have made to reach out thus far. Know that you are an aspect of God, connected to all that is and that each breath, each heartbeat, is an opportunity for you to serve the light, to become a master, to release hurt, pain, and darkness, transmuting them into a harmonious melody that resounds in the heavens. It is all your choice at any given moment to be an angel, walking as a human, serving all by being in love, and in truth, and so be it.

Layers

You are so dearly loved.

Each cycle presents a mystery that you are asked to solve. You desperately search for clues, when in fact you contain all the clues within you. You have the tools, as well as the necessary parts, to complete any puzzle asking to be solved. The clues hide within you and, when you invoke your memories, you realize that you are but revisiting the same situations you have been in before. Many of you believe that the movie you are acting in at the moment is new, but it is most likely not. We must impart to you that, too often, the drama you are experiencing is being invoked from scenes you have shot before. Each time a scene is revisited, you experience it differently, as it is recorded from angles representing views of the various actors. You are kept busy re-examining old takes from many perspectives. Your "light source" is continuously shifting, creating ever-changing shadows.

Why is it so, you may wonder?

Learning is complete only when you have been able to contemplate a lesson from all its angles. A violent life must, down the road, present lessons that offer opportunities to experience the perspective, not only of the perpetrator, but the perspective of the victim, as well. Karma is balanced when you have completed a full circle.

What mainly must change is not what you see or experience, but your own perspective, your own consciousness. Your vision is influenced by the way the light is refracted at the surface, the more the illumination presents, the more details you can see. In darkness you can hardly see anything. As light shines within your awareness, there is an offer to finally "deal" with what was hiding in the shadows. When your awareness becomes aligned with what you see, you are presented with a choice. That choice is a gift. Choices are simple to fathom but difficult to apply. You must choose between using love this time around, primarily love for self, extending to all, or not. Using anything but love inevitably redirects you back to the starting point so that you have an opportunity to do it all over again. Your choice is between acting in consciousness of the limited self or in the consciousness of the "I am." Acting from the "I am" releases you for all eternity from revisiting what was, while acting from the limited self-binds you for all eternity. This is the way of it. Eventually all become free on this eternal path to liberation.

Many of you believe that you are special; your circumstances are unique, that you are coping with whatever is in front of you for the very first time, that you are not ready, not equipped, not up to the task. In fact, almost all of you are mistaken on all of these accounts. Each time you are faced with a seemingly daunting task, know that, most likely, it is a continuation of a process that began at the edge of time in one of your many cycles as a physical being. Know that whatever is in front of you comes to you because you haven't completed that movie. Your previous experiences, whether conscious or not, are clues as to how you must proceed if you are to progress and advance through them.

How does it work, you may wonder?

Every possible potential, in your brief visit on the physical plane, had a beginning. It means that whatever happens to you was not arbitrary, but began as a potential when you began, which may have been when humanity was just in its infancy. Your "now" life is but the "tip of the iceberg," to use your phrase, of the many beginnings you have had over many cycles. All your lessons, experiences, trials and errors, are causes. Where you are now, and the billions of potentials that you have to choose from, are the effects. The cause, and the effects, are how your light progresses: a cosmic law that binds all. Each beginning created a movement of energy, which led to a new beginning. So much of your life is repeating your unfinished business. So much is already planned before you ever set your baby foot on this plane. It is, therefore, a sacred opportunity for many of you to be offered a door to exit your cause and effect cycle, gaining mastery over your movement, charting your own path, exploring new territories never before visited. Exciting it is for your being to get out of the groove of clearing unfinished business and to get initiated into open playing field; true freedom.

The storms swirling around you are meant to stir your unfinished business so you can see all that remains to be cleared, awaken, get out of your comfortable chair and go to work. By work we mean light-work. The work of creating light, clearing the old, and at times, graduating lessons of many cycles in one swoop. The time you knew as linear, minute two following minute one, is no longer. Gradually many of you sense that you exist both in the three-dimensional physical plane and also simultaneously existing in a multi-dimensional reality: a dimensional reality where beginnings, endings, and new beginnings, from various cycles crossing your path, colliding, intersecting with each other. This new reality swirls around you and shifts your "now" seemingly overnight. With a smile, we must add that it may be getting confusing for a while, as you are presented with a new paradigm, one with a multi-dimensional reality.

Am I ready? You ask.

Yes and no, we reply with yet another wink. You can never be truly ready because what you see is only the tip of the iceberg. Most of the movement and the reason for the movement is hidden, appearing, occasionally, in your peripheral vision. We wish to give you a simplified version, in physical terms, about that which we speak.

In the circle all movements occur simultaneously, and to translate this into your linear perception, we wish to break it down into metaphoric layers and begin with layer one.

In this layer you are moving into a new home.

In layer two you are moving into a new job, and in layer three, you are moving into new relationships.

In our present case, then, layer four, five, and six represent the challenges you face while dealing with layers one, two, and three. This may be called the extra factor, which can manifest as debilitating dis-ease, lack of funds, or looming threats of one kind or another.

Layers seven, eight, and nine are where you must deal with your elderly parents, your young children, while balancing yourself in the now. Metaphorically speaking, you are dealing with aspects of your past (seven), your infinite now (eight) and your future (nine).

The only constant is change and change is happening in an accelerated, unpredictable, and non-linear fashion.

Are you still surprised when you often feel depleted or exhausted, requiring more rest and quiet time than ever before? These layers are not new. What is new is the mechanics and synchronicity of these events, accelerating your progress by creating an expanded field of dimensional synergy, which then places added pressure on you.

Everyone has to deal with these layers. However, now, these layers are more demanding than ever because they show up for the purpose of clearing unfinished movies from old cycles. The challenge, metaphorically, is like moving in a hybrid vehicle, a combination of a mule, a boat, a car, and an airplane at the same time. You must grapple with various speeds, mechanics, and playing fields, yet remain intact—not a simple feat.

These layers are like shadows of the past. They appear, then disappear as quickly, once you have illuminated their essence by using love. As soon as one shadow is illuminated, a new shadow appears, all different, yet the same. All come from movies left unfinished. All movement seeks to find equilibrium before clearing away. Most of you are now in the midst of opening your dusty moldy attics, clearing away unfinished stories, some of which are very old. This is why you are now easily overwhelmed, as debris of all types, shapes, and sizes comes at you, seemingly from arbitrary directions. You are here in the now, clearing the past so you can move into a new future. Right there, you have three dimensions. Two are illusions, with your now moving so fast that you can hardly slow down enough to take a breath. This is your story and sacred it is.

Why are you sharing these stories? What good does it do to us?

You are energy moving through space and time. You sense that you are one wholesome being and you attempt to guard your wholesomeness, your oneness. Many feel threatened and bewildered by the forces of gravity that seemingly pull on you from all directions. Confusion this time, with the pressure on your system, is greater than you have ever known as a human on this planet. So many dimensions are working simultaneously. We share these stories with you so you do not feel that something is wrong with you. It is that simple. When you understand that this is the state of your field, you are more likely to act appropriately. You wished to ascend; you are now in the vortex of initiation into ascension. If you think for a moment that your challenges are to be over when you are in the ascension vortex, it is not so.

In the cosmos there are forces so great that a human can never grasp their power while in a body. There are beings of great light, there are beings of immense darkness. There is beauty, everywhere and life everywhere. Soon your definition of life will vastly change to include the inanimate as alive, within a defined field, vibrating and interacting with you in a conscious way. Your definition of consciousness must expand to see all as awakened, as that all vibrates and responds to conscious energy. Not the conscious way of a human, but still conscious.

You are now linked more intimately with a galactic stream of consciousness than ever before. Many of you who have moved high enough are taking part in a galactic conversation, which, in time, will grow to include every conscious being on this planet.

What is a galactic conversation and why should we care? You ask.

Your field expands far beyond your planetary borders and is now overlapping and coinciding with fields of other galactic consciousness. The magnetic fields are strong enough and sufficiently coherent to be called a conversation. It is so because the communication taking place is immediate, clear, precise, and intended.

Why do we care?

You are changing, your reality is changing, your cells are changing, your planet is changing, your magnetic field is changing, your atmosphere is changing, your natural habitat is changing; your weather is changing. Every pattern that has been there for millennia and determined the way you interact with your world is changing. If you walk in a dark path, hurting yourself each time you bump into something you did not expect, then, someone offered you a flashlight, wouldn't you take the offer? Would you still wonder, why should I care?

Those of you who were meant to read our words most likely are aware of these changes. You have cleared enough weight and become sufficiently subtle to where small changes in the magnetic field around you get recorded in your body and affect the way you feel. If you do not know what these changes mean, you may grow anxious or become a hypochondriac, worrying why you feel the way you do. The changes in your magnetic field are extreme by our standards and so many of you find it challenging just keeping up. Some develop health challenges expressed as cellular mutations and various misalignments. You cannot resist these changes and if you attempt to stop the clearing movement, you will only harm your integrity and equilibrium. We wish you to learn to float like a leaf on a raging river knowing that you will be guided to where you need to be without stirring. To many, action is your main focus and you wish to get things done. We ask you to get out of your own way, become peaceful, and so, surrendering to what is. Your main task is to align with your truth moving in unison with your field, causing as little dissonance as possible.

Water flows with ease around blocks and obstacles. The forces of gravity dictate its path. Water will always flow in accordance with the terrain most harmonious with the guiding natural laws. Like water, you are now being guided to move higher in your evolutionary path as spirit manifested in the physical. Resisting this evolutionary path is like water trying to flow uphill rather than streaming to the valley.

What is it that you are asking from us?

Slow down; consult your heart in everything that you do, trust. Act in accordance with your truth. Be precise; be honest with self.

With each breath and heartbeat, intend to create a movement out from your heart, remaining awake even when it feels uncomfortable. Surrender, flow, and accept, allowing your power to flow from the admonition that forcing is going against self. Breathe, knowing that with each inhalation you become one with the whole and with each exhalation the whole becomes one with you. Acknowledge that any and all forms of resistance are generated from within.

This is just the foundation. On top of the foundation you must build your vehicle.

Which parts should we use to build it? You ask.

There are three aspects to the structure being built on top of the foundation. It looks like three spheres of magnetic fields interacting with your physical body. The first sphere is guided by your breath, the second field is guided by your heartbeat, and the third field is guided by your senses. Slowing your breath, calming, and becoming aware of your heartbeat will cause your senses to automatically align with the current now-state that you must be in, in order to perceive your reality through the most conducive channel to act appropriately. Acting appropriately carries no judgment and no polarity. Appropriateness means that your energy is aligning with the vibrational resonance of your changing environment and not in discord. The more harmonic your vibration is, the more your resonance with your planetary field is enhanced; your feeling of well-being expands, resulting in more love that you absorb and can project. Acting in dissonance with the planetary field means that each day you will feel disconnected from self, from love, from the galactic melody, and from the trajectory of your charted path toward growth. When you are in discord, you are not in the vortex of alignment and your body may let you know by going against itself. Cells against cells, an immune system which attacks healthy cells. Autoimmune and cancerous cells are cells that are not with the program. It happens more frequently as the electromagnetic baseline you were accustomed to shifts ever more rapidly.

What practical steps can we take? You wonder.

There is an angelic entourage assigned to you. There are angel beings around you, who are available to guide your every step. There are signs and guideposts placed in front of you every day. Many of you, dare we say most of you, ignore the signs, muffle the voices of your entourage, and keep going until you fall. Once you fall, some of you are forced to slow down just enough to read the signs. When you get better, most go back to ignoring the signs until you are faced with a dead end and then, dear human angel; it is too late in this cycle to shift. When you reach a dead end, you see all the things you have chosen to ignore, all the signs that were placed for you to read, the writing on the walls, to use your Earthly expression, but, at this point, you cannot change much, only understand and accept. Life is precious; your life is the most precious aspect of your journey. Every breath is a gift. Every daylight shines your path. We ask you to open your eyes and celebrate the fact that you have been given the most sacred opportunity in many cycles: to chart your own destiny in a manner that was not possible before; experiencing reality as a multidimensional galactic being. Moving into your vortex, being in your truth, you begin to experience reality from a place of fearlessness, trust, and joy, seeing beauty and appropriateness every which way you turn. What once seemed to be dark and daunting is being illuminated from within you. You no longer see dark as bad or as a threat; you see dark as simply lack of light, with no power of its own. When you come near this darkness, you light it up with your own inner illumination and it vanishes forever. This is your call to duty and it is why we love you so. We ask you to use your tools so you can help build a bridge so that many may cross to a new reality now being created, and so be it.

Into the Fire

You are so dearly loved!

It is with great pleasure that we are here, yet again, holding you, hugging you, loving you, reassuring you that all is unfolding in perfect order. The timing of each major event in your life is meticulously planned. No one has the ultimate access key to the Akashic records where the plans are being stashed, although at times you get glimpses of what is to unfold. Your choices invoke the potential that eventually plays out. All potentials waiting in those records are ready to be activated when the time is "right." You are on a visit to a dimension that is dense, coming for such a brief moment, and you already leave. Some of you have much to accomplish. It makes sense that there is very little down time between adventures. Many complain that, while one adventure ends, another begins. It is so because there is a purpose, a direction, and even logic, not linear but spiritual logic, to the main events presented in your life. There is no waste and no stopping to your growth and learning. Only your wish to stop growing will slow you down, yet the pressure to grow will remain. When you choose to stop growing you are no longer aligned with your purpose here in this dimension. Your contract spells growth and expansion; awakening and learning.

You ask, *how come I cannot find any logic on my path and lots of challenges*?

The logic is of the "I am" and it is not linear, nor does it abide by your three-dimensional rules of cause and effect. The law of cause and effect indeed plays out, where causes from, not any single, but many lifetimes manifest the effect. You may experience a collision of effects as intense, challenging scenarios, often within short periods of time, offering you a rich and complex playground for growth and creation. Sacred expansion can be achieved within a relatively short period of time during these collision events or "big bangs."

Your soul family, whether physical, spiritual, natural, or adopted, is what we call the "goldmine" for challenges and your greatest source for profound growth and expansion.

Why is it so, you ask?

The ones who are closest to you reflect you to yourself in the most direct way. Your closest circle, or what we call your soul family, has been with you most likely in past lives and will keep coming in future ones. Past and future are only but a dream, so that the now you are living at this moment, breath by breath, heartbeat by heartbeat, sounds out the melody of all your lives, past and future, uniting them into a moment in time. Your family brings to you many unfinished stories as they ask you to make peace with those stories. You do not need to solve anything, but to find neutral grounds, so that these stories will no longer hold the energy of an unfinished affair. Love is the adhesive that keeps the story going. The emotional energy gives you the incentive to resolve what needs to be resolved. You cannot walk away from soul family like you may walk away from your outer circle of friends or co-workers. With your soul family, the bond is always there. Even when you ignore the contract and pretend it does not exist, you are always connected to those who make up your soul family circle.

Beneath the ocean there are amazing creatures. One must be equipped for diving to be able to see those creatures and appreciate their magnificence. On a boat, the ocean seems to be just a surface in motion. Only when you dive into it and become immersed in it, do you begin to access its full glory.

When you are born into the human family you are like a captain of a ship and you see only the surface of the ocean. Your family is your diving equipment. It gives you access so you may immerse yourself in the depth and full meaning of being human.

You are a magnificent being: a being that comes from the stars, and dresses up for a moment as a human, so you may have access to this sacred school for growth, expansion, love, and beauty. The points of access to all of the above are through your soul family.

You may ask yourself, so why is this family so dysfunctional? Why must it be so painful? Why must it hold so many challenges?

Reflect and contemplate your circumstances and you will see that all events, which involve your closest soul family, stem from love. Love is the bond, the adhesive, the tool that spirit uses to immerse you deeper than you would ever go if you didn't care.

I do not understand. You complain. *Why am I to go into such intense emotional states just to find ways to neutralize their intensity?*

With all love, so much of your spiritual journey on this dimension is counterintuitive. The reason is simple: the process of neutralizing intense emotional states can only be done through love. Within your culture many resort to medicating themselves, but this, unfortunately, does not neutralize the emotional state. It only camouflages its signs, often delaying your progress. Indeed, many are being assisted in overcoming debilitating emotional challenges in their lives and that is sacred. But, used as a tool, it will not offer a lasting path for growth. Medication only, then, cannot create a lasting change in the geometry and light structure of the soul.

In all aspects of creation, if only logic would have played out, your story would be too predictable, too shallow, and would not require you to have faith, to learn to trust, to exercise love toward self and others. If each action would lead you to a predictable reaction, your life would feel like a two-dimensional cartoon with limited transformative power. The journey of an angel dressed up as a human is to go into the fire and emerge intact. The only power that can motivate you to walk into the fire is love. The only power that can lead you safely and intact out of the fire is love. Your soul family is your main tool to teach you about love from all angles. It is a framework for learning. If you were not in school would you spend much of your waking hours completing your homework? Your soul family is your school and it presents you with an incentive to do your homework.

Some of my family members are not showing me love. The more I try the worse it gets. What am I doing wrong? You ask.

Dear human, you are not doing anything wrong. There is really no wrong in these set ups. You have your stage and you have the actors. Each plays their part. Your role is to radiate oneness and the other's role is to express duality. All has a place. Know that even when all seems to be off, there is spiritual logic running through, leading and directing all the actors towards growth.

You have come this far. You walked through fire and you emerged intact, whole, and beautiful. We shed tears of joy when one transforms from lead to gold through alchemy. To become purer one must burn, shed, and discard all that is impure. By pure we mean your core, your truth, your soul essence, and the beauty of your light. Flying requires clearing all the extra weight. Ascending requires eliminating the excess baggage that does not belong to you. Anything and everything that is not emanating from love and does not serve your highest path must be purified. The past guides you to move closer to self.

Who do you think you are? We ask.

You see yourself in terms of an individual who is trying to do the right thing. We see you as a unique sound vibration, a melody, we see you in terms of colors and in term of light. We do not see you the way you see yourself. We see you in terms of your purpose. Being aligned with your purpose requires you to be truthful and to reside in your heart. The more aligned you are with your truth, the brighter your luminosity, the more harmonious your melody, the more vibrant are your colors. The story that you tell yourself is only a small part of your movie. You come here to penetrate the surface of the ocean; you come here to dive into the depth of the human experience and when you emerge, your hands full of pearls, shining and reflecting their brilliance in the sun's rays, you have discovered your treasure and aligned to your purpose. Your task is to seek your truth and, in the process, shed what is not you, letting go of attachments which do not serve you, discarding outfits which are not your size, and clearing debris which only clutters your home.

How do I know what is mine and what isn't, you ask?

You are love, your core is of love. The way you find your core is by connecting to your heart, allowing it to guide you. When you are disconnected from your heart, you are not fulfilling your purpose.

Why love, you ask?

Love is spirit and love is God. Love is the substance, which connects all that is. You have many tasks to fulfill, but the most important one is to find love, first for yourself and then from this core self to all. No love to others is ever transformative when one is not in a place of self-love. All your challenges carry but one common denominator, discovery of self-love.

Why is it so challenging and illusive, some inquire?

With a smile, we ask you, why does a two-year-old not stay a two-year-old? Self-love is no more elusive than a two-year-old is elusive. Both must grow up, change, shift, expand, and transform. Self-love is the key to your evolution. Living your truth and being a source of light to others is your purpose. A planet inhabited by angels who know their power, carrying in them the seeds of self-love, sprouts the foundation of the new reality.

Each time you encounter a challenge, know that behind the story there is always love and behind the word love you are challenged to discover the treasure of self-love. There is no greater challenge facing all of you assigned to manifesting the new bridge of light, now being built, than self-love. When you face core learning, know that your external reality will present to you a mirror reflection of your learning. When self-love is your core prize this cycle, it means that you are nearing graduation and all the lessons not yet resolved, where love of self and honoring of self were not present, may come up now in your life. When a mirror image of self-love is being presented, it appears as the opposite image. Know that hate, anger, rejection, betrayal, violence, or abuse are but mirror reflections of self-love. There is nothing more sacred and profound for an angel than to find its own light. Only when you have found your light, may you show the road to others.

Where are we going, you ask?

Many of you have gone through challenging initiations and you know now that you can walk through fire and emerge intact. Now is the time to emerge, to come out of your cocoons, and spread your butterfly wings. Share your colors, your beauty, and fear not. You now know your power, your commitment, and your tenacity. You know that you came to explore self-love, living your light and truth. When you discover God within, you radiate a field of energy that is enormous in size. It is being felt in the far reaches of the cosmos. We ask you to celebrate, dance, and find pleasure in each other; in yourself; in your vessel. You are now graduating the lesson of fear, transforming it to fearlessness; the lesson of doubt, transforming it to trust. You have labored to become light and it is your time to spread your wings. You are ready and all the work that you have done is paying off. The split that we spoke of has occurred, the storms that we spoke of have occurred, the joyride that we spoke of has occurred. It is time to practice being, no longer becoming, but being. When you are in the knowledge that all is complete, you are ready to move into a new state of reality, which is the state of being. Your heart is pumping blood to your body not because you will it but because it listens to your autonomic nervous system, which instructs it to do just that. You are now shifting from willing to being, from manifesting to dreaming, from having to containing, from achieving to existing in a place of love. You have graduated one lesson and moved on to the next. One was full of challenges and the other is of mastery. Master the art of "being," knowing full well that whatever crosses your path is there for you to eventually lead you to self-love.

We are you, we love you, and so be it.

Reboot

Yes, you are *still* dearly loved.

Beautiful human angel, if you just knew, deep in your heart, the care and sacredness that went into the planning of every moment in your current cycle you would be awestruck. The planning committee is made out of you, your angels, the teachers, the consultants, and guides; the advisors and all are just different names for the group that makes up who you are. You take up one body with billions of parts. You are one soul with many facets. You, however, are never separated from the great central sun, some call God.

We come to you, yet once again, to break down the mechanics of your path so you can awaken to the process and enjoy the ride. Much is riding on you relaxing, being present, connected to your heart, and, in gratitude, not giving into worry or fear. We ask you to awaken so you would "see" that all aspects of your life serve a purpose. Your purpose is growth. We are messengers of light and we speak to those who are holding the torches this time around. The torch holder's purpose is to create a bridge of light for others who are awakening themselves. Yet, there are those who work with the dark. All has its place. It is not our place to work with darkness but know that dark serves a purpose as well. We ask you to shine light because this is how you progress. Your essence is love and your heart is the light bulb. The less resistance you carry within you, the greater your energy output; the brighter your luminosity. There is never a judgment placed on how far you go and how much light you shine. All your choices are sacred and being honored. Your wholeness is part of the one. We wish you to know that there is only gain, and nothing to lose, being in your truth, aligned with your purpose.

What are you searching for? We ask.

I am looking for myself, we hear you say.

Why are you then venturing so far? What is waiting for you out there that you do not already have?

I am looking for meaning; the meaning to my life.

A fish must find its purpose within the bounds of water. You must find your purpose within the rim of your heart.

There are three aspects of your growth that are outside of you.

What are they? You ask.

With a smile, we answer: heaven, Earth and everything in between.

Funny, then, everything is outside of me?

Yes and no.

Please explain.

You must have context for your movement. The setting always appears to be outside of you, yet, the movement is always inside of you. As you walk on Earth, the context is continuously changing. All you have to do is take a walk in the park and observe the shifting scenery. The framework of your circumstances is there to serve your growth and not the opposite. Heaven, Earth, and everything in between is there to guide you. These three aspects, outside of you, yet they contain you. You are one with them. Everything that you experience through your physical reality is only a reflection of the external projected on the internal, and that reflection creates a movement within you. There is really nothing outside of you but currents of energy, fluctuating and vibrating. You are a hologram and you contain within you the entire three aspects; seen and unseen. You contain the whole, yet separate from it because you can perceive it.

We wish to speak with you about an aspect of your journey, which many of you encounter, to some degree.

When a car swerves off its course, hitting you, and you get injured, your external aspect and internal aspect have just collided. The result of the collision, besides the obvious pain and medical treatment that you must undergo, is that your external and internal vibrational field align for a moment. You may call it rebooting (borrowing the term from your computer technology). Difficult, challenging, even traumatic events in your life, ones that carry the potential to change your entire life trajectory and make you reevaluate everything and everyone in your life, are what we are referring to as "reboots."

Your external aspect or reality, at times, must collide with your inner state or reality, so a movement can occur which shocks you, leaving you with an intense imprint for a moment. This imprint may last, at times, for only a moment, but at other times it may last for a day, for a month, for a year, or a lifetime. This event is recognized by the soul as a temporary alignment. When the soul creates a set up for a "reboot," it means one of two things: it may mean an upgrade of your vibration to the next level, or, the other possibility is, that your external and internal aspects have drifted so far apart that the soul must take extreme measures to realign heaven, Earth, and everything in between, to your inner reality. The "reboot" often melds the outer circumstance with the inner via an orchestrated event so the imprint creates a temporary unified sphere of reality and, therefore, an alignment. Shortly following the alignment there is no more separation, no diversions, and no doubts. For a moment, heaven, Earth, and everything in between is reflected by the one being, rebooted, melding all disparity between the outer and inner "realities." This is a sacred event, one that is planned far in advance. This potential is known before you ever descend to Earth's dimension through the birth canal.

Why does it matter, you ask?

You come here to grow, develop, and align with your truth. You create light by being aligned, when you are lost without a candle, you are just lost. When you become so lost, you have no access to your entourage, and you are mainly sailing to where the winds of fear, doubts, and reactive survival take you, with no regard as to where your destined shore may be. When all that you know to be your world comes to a momentary standstill, and you must drop whatever you were doing in your life and deal with "that" which in front of you, you may be experiencing a system reset; a sacred movement chosen by your "I am" to guide you higher. This sacred process often allows you to momentarily remember who you are, why you came here, and what your purpose is, this time around.

Why are you telling us about all this?

Next time you experience an event that stops you in your tracks, giving you an opportunity to reevaluate everything you have been doing up until that point in your life, you will know what to name it: a reboot.

Naming is easy but what do we do next, you ask?

Most of you will try to find a way to go back to where you have been before. Even though it did not serve you, caused you pain, made you miserable, and confused you, at least you knew what to expect. When your system has been "re-booted," know that there is no going back to the old you. Even if you try, you are bound to not be able to find that old self. It has been reset. If you try and try, you may recreate the same old self; go back to where it felt comfortable, and, by then, the soul may give up trying and allow you to fall asleep, until it is time for your cycle to end. Many people are in that place. The growth has ceased and they are in a holding place until the biology quits. Then, the soul gets another reboot, this time using a different name, body, and circumstances. The learning never ends. Your soul's desire to grow never tires, your journey is eternal and the question you may wish to ask yourself: *why sleep, when being awake offers so much beauty.*

You are given choices at every intersection on your journey. One of those choices is there to serve your expanded "I am" and align with your truth. Often it is presented as the less desirable or more challenging choice.

Why is it so? Why not make it so obvious and the easiest one to pick, you ask?

You came here to learn and grow, that is why. In a test, are you being asked all the questions you already know the answers to? Same with your "I am." You create circumstances, which require you to stretch your abilities, to overcome your fears, to battle your darkness, and to face your karma. None of those choices would be considered easy, but all of them serve your expanded "I am" purpose in taking a body and merging heaven, Earth, and all that is in between, with you, the chariot of light. There is an active ingredient in each choice selection that may give you an indication to which door is open to growth and which isn't.

What is this active ingredient, you ask?

Resistance, of course—if there is no resistance would there be any growth? Like air to a bird and water to fish, a human angel requires resistance to fly. Look for that resistance as an opportunity to reexamine your choices. At times the opposition is justified, and, at times, it may be only your own resistance to grow, fueled by fear, lack of self-esteem, lack of self-confidence, or lack of courage. When you are terrified of something and you cannot sleep at night because of a fear of failing and not making it, know that it may be your soul asking you to take that step, because this is why you are here. To walk, to take plunges, and to move through fear.

What if the resistance is justified and I can get myself in trouble by choosing to take risks?

When you consult your heart and set an intention to grow with love and light, you eliminate the dark choices. Know that you are not coming to this dimension to win, you come here to play the game.

The game is played by you, being you, connected to your expanded "I am." If you are not aligned with your truth, you are sitting on the bench. Your ego wants the results, but the soul doesn't care about results, as she wants you to be in the game. Participating is winning. When you are walking your walk, no award and no recognition can come close to the trophy you earn by being in your truth.

Know that your angelic entourage, the one who never leaves you alone, thrives on challenges. We wish you to know that whatever you choose, you are loved just the same. We know why you are here. We are with you from before you were born into a body and after what you consider as "death" of the physical body. In our realm you were never born and you will never die, but we are with you throughout your physical cycle and we wish you to know that we love it when you keep us busy. The only time that we cannot reach you is when you have given up completely and stop playing the game. We ask you to play, allowing your heart to lead and your light to guide you to where you need to be. And so be it.

Gratitude

Thank you for being you. You are dearly loved.

Gratitude is the keyword to enter the realm of spirit. Why is this so? Because you are a vehicle for spirit. The more balanced you are, the spirit within you can follow its truth and drives your vehicle to its highest path. The true union of spirit with its vehicle begins and ends with gratitude. Spirit honors the vehicle allowing its expression and the human acknowledgment of the sacredness hosting spirit within its physicality. The mutual gratitude is what feeds the light within this divine union. Being in gratitude is always within the range of choices you have and is the choice, which catapults any reality into its most elevated expression. The movement is instant and it affects all fields of existence within you, around you, extending to the universe.

The power of true gratitude is in its shape. It is shaped like a tetrahedron key. This key opens the gate to true knowing, to true surrender, and to a true acceptance of this union. Spirit wishes to express itself; the ego within the physical vehicle wishes to express itself; the body wishes to express itself. All expressions are in balance only when the entire being is in gratitude. You do not come here to embody one hundred percent spirit. You do that when you are not in a body. You do not come here to embody one hundred percent of your being as an expression of the ego, if that would be the case you would no longer have Earth as your home. You would not have balance between light and dark. There would be no light in a reality that is driven by ego only. You also do not come here to embody your physical vehicle at one hundred percent. If that would be the case, you would not seek spirit. You would only eat drink, sleep, and procreate.

Your journey is about merging the three elements into one. Many of your religions knew of these aspects and called them by different names. Many esoteric traditions attempted to find ways to merge the three into one balanced human. Very few have succeeded in teaching balance. For the human to be balanced she has to be free. Free, that is, from shame, guilt, anger, resentment, fear, jealousy, possessiveness, greed, or hate, which represent attributes of imbalance within the three. When you are not in balance, your reality is viewed through the imbalance; it becomes your "truth." The more balanced you are, the more balanced reality becomes. Gratitude is the key tonal frequency that is powerful enough to realign an incoherent oscillation of chaotic agitated frequencies into a coherent resonance and to shift, instantly, your reality towards balance.

Many of you, who call yourself spiritual, place emphasis on quieting the ego and putting your physical vehicle to sleep, so your spirit can be the conductor and the music played will be played to its tune.

This, though, is as much an imbalance, as it would be if the ego had the seat of the conductor, or as if the physical vehicle did.

Why is it so? Some may ask. *We thought you wished spirit to be the leader.*

True spirit is not a leader; spirit is an expression, it is love. True spirit does not need to dominate; it needs to merge all aspects of your humanness so that the dye of spirit stains every energetic expression that you emit through action, thoughts, or feelings.

When spirit overtakes the other two elements that make you a human, it becomes a distortion and it may cause harm or pain, and is in the realm of darkness.

When a human angel deprives itself of her humanness, it is not in the realm of light. When a human angel deprives its body of honoring the sacredness of its expression and pleasure, its spectrum of luminosity is in the dark shades of gray.

Light is honoring the entirety of you, every cell that makes you who you are. When vibrating with gratitude you are whole, leading you to your highest vibration, love. Love is the doorway to spirit; gratitude is the key to that doorway.

When a human angel seeks to destroy her ego, she is diminished from the "I am" to just "I." If you seek to erase the "I" there is only "am." Being solely "am" is existing without light; being solely the "I" is existing without spirit. "I am," then, is the marriage between your physical expression and spirit. It is the inclusion of all your aspects into one light being.

Those who extinguish their "I," and slaughter their "dragon" (ego) do away with their fire and no longer play a role in the realm of human angels. They have placed themselves on the bench. More often than not, it is a strategy to avoid experiencing painful feelings buried in one's humanness. When you euthanize self, you stop your suffering, but you also stop your humanness from being expressed. You have extinguished your light by erasing the "I" from the "I am."

The body has been depicted as a vehicle of sin in many of your traditions. The so-called "vices" are often the expression of the needs of the body. Many of your religious and traditional laws were put in place to curb your physical needs and redirect your physical energy that you would otherwise express through your body towards spiritual growth. This misguided understanding of the balance is the cause to some of the most horrific events Earth has witnessed and grounds for the darkest expression of religions. The imbalance caused by suppressing one element of your humanness, in an attempt to artificially create a larger opening within spirit, actually does the opposite. It corrupts both elements and creates a distortion between your physical aspect and your spiritual aspect. Physical pleasure deprivation has been redirected into a distortion of pleasure sensed within the realm of spirit; "I" deprivation creates a fertile ground for immense atrocities expressed as the will of the masses, where the sense of the self (ego) is decimated and the energy of the multitude takes the front seat, directing an entire group of one kind against an entire group of another kind. The "I" is no longer in its core power, but has been vaporized and swallowed by the "we," therefore no longer having a conscious say in what takes place. When the "I" is no longer in the game, powers with enough potency to will their wishes can use the diminished "I's" to bring about unimaginable darkness-manifested evil. Each imbalance has its own price to pay.

The first and last step of integrating your three elements into one is gratitude. Gratitude opens the gate to self-love; self-love opens the gate to wholesome love. The gratitude is for who you are, for what you appear to be in your physical form, for the light that you bring, and for the beauty that emanates from you; the gratitude is for the ground you step on, the air you breathe, for the challenges you face, and for those who bring forth these challenges; the gratitude is, also, for being given this time to be in physical form, expressing, and re-uniting your core spiritual self with your physical vehicle; finally, the gratitude is for being given the opportunity to manifest a bridge to cross over to the realm of the "I am," where your entirety becomes the expression of the human angel, walking your true path, balanced.

Each time you choose to hold back one of your three aspects; it is as if you have removed one of the angles of a tetrahedron. When all three are holding their balanced equal share, your core is powerful. When one of the corners is overtaken by an imbalance you are in an agitated state.

We love you and there is never a judgment, from our side on your placement, in the continuum of growth in your current journey. Know that, whenever one side of the tetrahedron is imbalanced, you may choose to re-balance it on your next visit to the physical dimension by over-growing the weaker angle. Deprivation or other extreme measures on either the spiritual, physical, or the ego "I," must find equilibrium over lifetimes. When all three are in balance the epic ascends and this movement becomes more and more subtle toward reuniting with the great "I am."

Why are you telling us about gratitude and how is it connected to the tetrahedron?

Tetrahedron is the shape of gratitude. It holds the geometry of balance and equilibrium. We are you and you asked us to shine light on your journey. One way is to shine light on simple tools, which give you enough energy to hold still and find balance in the midst of chaos and agitations.

You asked to grow wings. The higher you fly, the more anchored to Earth you must be. The wider you venture, the more connected to your core you must be. Venturing far without knowing who you are may leave you lost, confused, and in darkness. The more spiritual you wish to grow, the more grounded in your body you must be. The more spiritual you wish to be, the friendlier you must be with your ego, the "I." For ascension of your frequency to take place, you must have all three angles of the tetrahedron in balance. You see, your humanness cannot be avoided, your body cannot be ignored, and your spirituality cannot be hidden. For you to merge all the fragmented you's into a wholesome human angel you must use the key to open the gate, the key that is gratitude.

You are an angel, you are a human, and you are biology. Pleasure is your key to your biology; love is your key to the ego, your "I," and gratitude is your key to spirit. When gratitude embraces all of the "you's," you are it, and so be it.

The Player

Yes, indeed, you are loved.

Do you doubt? Do you hesitate? Do you wonder or question? Do you stumble, get hurt and cry? Yet, do you move through it all and emerge? Do you see the light in all of it?

If the answer is yes to all these questions, indeed, you are awakening.

Do you see now, looking back, that you have been being guided all along on this path? Each turn is a brushstroke, laid on a masterpiece in progress. Each test holds a mystery and a puzzle; each leap you have taken moves you deeper, guiding you back to your heart, your life, humanity, and to your truth; to love, to light, to the great "I am." Contemplating where your angelic self begins and your human self ends is like contemplating which clouds you like the best. Since there is a constant transformation, movement, and shifting, the clouds appear one way and a moment later, another. You are an angel and the shape that you take, while walking Earth's dimension, is merely a melody that follows your dance. Your dance is always heavenly. Your next step is one of surrender to your purpose, your mission, your truth. Allow yourself to be led by the hand, like the child guided by her mother across a busy intersection. It is indeed a time for you to slow down and make every movement, and every breath, count. Make every intention clear and each choice heart-based. There is little room for negotiation. The razor thin edge you are walking, demands that you focus, not looking down and not allowing your thoughts to distract your heart. Know that, the higher you climb, the less room you have to tread, let alone to allow for wondering. We have shared with you since 2007 that all that you experience is a choice, and, at each intersection, you do choose: light or dark, left or right. At times when you choose dark, subsequent choices no longer offer light, but shades of gray. There are some who, at one junction or another of their cycle, choose darkness. They have strayed far away from their truth and from love; their lower self overcame their higher self, shading their light so they could satisfy the insatiable hunger of the lower emotions and their ego. Some may have chosen a dance, at one juncture, that painted their energy field with heavy dark colors. There is never a judgment as to the choices you make, but know that it may take lifetimes to clear your field from the residual effect of one single choice. Artists make choices as to what is being applied on the surface of their canvas. Once the choice has been made, it becomes part of the identity and energy makeup of that angel and the masterpiece being birthed.

Why is it so?

The higher you climb, the more "impactful" is the fall. It is the law of gravity. If you are a baby, you may climb up on a chair, but then, if you fall, you may well bruise and scratch yourself a little. When you are a mountain climber who aspires to touch the sky, when you fall, it might be fatal to your body. There is never a judgment on this side of the veil. It may be that you get so close to the apex, to graduating from one concentric circle to the next, spiraling ever upward, and then you make a choice which lands you all the way back to circle one. What it means is that your personality was not mature enough to graduate one vibration and move on to the next. You were guided to reach a junction where all your hard-earned qualities had to join together and guide you through to make a choice with light and with love. At the higher elevation these choices are never easy and could be testing your limits. The motivation for a choice is as important as the choice itself. The more aware you become, the narrower your path becomes, and the less tolerance your "I am" is for choices not aligned with your knowing. If you made a choice out of fear, out of insecurity, out of arrogance, sense of superiority, ego, you may have chosen darkness. Darkness is not necessarily evil, yet, it could be. Choosing darkness may not be intentional, yet it might be. It may not be directed at someone, yet it can be. When one chooses to intentionally hurt another with full awareness, it is an action, which does not leave much negotiating room in which the soul may maneuver. Great spiritual leaders have been tested, at their peak, and condemned by history for all time. Why? Because they knew better. It is not history that you must be concerned with; it is the knowing of the "I am" living with the consequences of your actions. Anger, betrayal, hate, desire for revenge, are all lower emotions. Compassion, gratitude, and forgiveness are emotions emanating from love. Love neutralizes the lower emotions and paves a path to move higher. The one, who chooses to allow the lower self to overtake the higher self, made their pick. Once the choice was made one may need to start over, renegotiating a lower-self life back up. Like a soul Monopoly, at times you may need to go a few steps backward and start over. However, in this "game" the dice's number is chosen by you. The path higher is not for the meek, it is for the warriors. A warrior must face their dragons, must expose their inner monsters to light, and must battle their demons, to progress. A warrior must be willing to "die." Once the warrior surrenders to their demons, they are no longer warriors of light, as they become instruments of the dark. You are all alchemists, magicians of sorts. Dark magicians hold power that is void of love; white magicians possess powers that radiate love. Transparent magicians moved away from duality and no longer in the game, they oversee the game from a place of detachment and are always in light. Knowledge is a double-edged sword, when you climb to merge with your God-self. There is less and less tolerance for excuses, for ambiguity, for laziness, for indecisiveness. When you hold the power of heart-light knowledge in your hand and then you veer from what you know is love-based, allowing your lower self to be in the driver's seat, do you really believe that, somehow, no one will notice?

It takes many lifetimes for an angel to climb up; to change, emerging from the cocoon of fear of survival, ignorance, prejudice, cultural programming, from un-evolved parental and societal dispositions. We have focused on those of you who chose to awaken, reuniting with their power, their light, and their inner sanctuary. You are the warriors, the giants, walking about in everyday clothing, pretending to be regular, yet are anything but. It is time to look at those on the other side, the angels who wish for power and control; to conquer; making up the ones we call dark.

Many of the dark ones were once of the light. They were just like you on the path, they were moving along their trajectory and attracted the attention of the dark by demonstrating their proclivity to manipulate energy and with abilities like charisma, determination, and perseverance. At times, it requires but one, well-aimed, gust of wind to puff out one's candle.

And so we ask you to guard your light. Become aware and beware while making choices based on lower emotions; wait, feel, allow your emotions to subside. When you face a choice that involves a tumultuous emotional storm, being silent, and not acting, can lift you very high. Giving in to the lower emotion may drag you to depths that may take lifetimes from which to reemerge. There is never a judgment from this side of the veil as there is never any end to this journey. Wherever you are on this endless track to reunite with your God-self, is honored.

There is no rush. You are, after all, an eternal angel. And yet, please know that tests do get more challenging the higher your climb. Your integrity, your truth, your alignment with your heart, with compassion, with love is not measured by anything societal, it is measured, from within, by your inner self, your all-knowing self your "I am." It is not like having some patrolman catch you speeding and give you a ticket but, if you did manage to drive ninety miles an hour, with no radar in sight, you will make it into the clear. This is not how it works with spirit. No one is policing you except you yourself. You cannot hide your thoughts, feelings, and actions from the "I am." It is all-knowing, and regardless of what everyone thinks about you, your God-self knows, and it will ask you to account for your choices, to face your lower self. You can be the most sophisticated player, who can hide your true self from everyone, playing the game of light to perfection, but you cannot hide from your "I am." Your higher aspect, the one who guides you along the trajectory, higher and higher, knows who you are, and, with love, and through love, will have you face yourself. There is no escaping the speeding traffic police because the judge, jury, and plaintiff are all within you. Using the language of light is like using any language, it requires knowledge and the ability to manipulate energy, however, being light, is different than using the language of light. Being light requires no talent, no knowledge, and no manipulation. It requires you to move with integrity, truth, love, compassion, gratitude, and forgiveness, and to acknowledge when you are not. It is the path of the warrior to look at yourself unflinching, and to forgive yourself.

Some of you believe that you can fool yourselves by pretending to be one way, while acting another way. You know who you are, and when you act like in shadow, while claiming to represent the light, it may fool people. You may attract followers, yet, your higher self will know and, at some point, you will need to answer to your "I am."

Karma cannot be manipulated, it is pure; it is a cosmic law that applies to anyone and everyone. You may claim that you did not know and use excuses, but your higher aspect knows. Some who chose to be of the light became dark, because, in darkness, you can gain power, manipulate energy, and it is allowed, under free will, universal protection. When one chooses to be in shadow, its higher self disengages from the process. The dark does not need to answer to anyone. Its lower aspect controls its path. If and when, at some point, the higher self re-engages in the process, as it must to merge with the greater God-self, then all the actions hidden from sight resurface and replay in the life of that human. Do you still wonder why some of you experience lives that are arduous, challenging, saturated with pain and misery, while other's lives are not? Karma does not skip over anything. It is not a punishment; it is the path all angels must follow to merge with God, with the "I am." You have been told that God sees all and it is true because God is you, and you see all that you think, feel, and act upon. We are angels and we are a part of you. You are never judged by anyone in the spirit world as harshly as you are judged by yourself. Your mentors, guides, elders, and entourage are a compassionate, grateful bunch who supports you no matter what you do or how you choose to act. Your higher self is the one who chooses your lessons, and your karmic path.

The ultimate choice is always yours and you have your guides, the circle of seven, the nine guardians, the elders, the angels around you, acting as advisors, suggesting the way, but it is you, my dear angel, who are the ultimate boss.

The darker the shade you take, the more arduous the road back. This is why, at times, the dark stays in the dark for many lifetimes. It is just easier. Why you may ask?

It delays the process of acknowledgment, awakening, and atonement. It suspends that process. Being in darkness disengages the higher aspect, allowing you to play the game without moving any closer to your God-self. You may still enjoy life like anyone else, but it is not aligned to your purpose, and not linked to your higher self. Some of you may look at those who are in the dark and say to themselves, "They have it good, why am I having it so hard, yet they are celebrating?"

Just wait; once they make the choice to link with the light, which must happen at some point on the soul's evolutionary trajectory, everything they have done will surface to be reconciled. No stone will remain unturned in that process. It may take many lifetimes for one in darkness to reignite their light and clear away their past actions. Know that the higher your climb, the more challenging the tests become.

Yet, there is no need to fear the tests. Just remember that light is truth, and that your inner light knows all about your truth. There are those who believe that they can lie to everyone; that it's safe to mislead anyone, anytime, yet their higher self will always know the difference. You are all loved by your angels. We hold your hands regardless of your choices. We are of light and we do not judge you when you choose darkness. We always keep the torch illuminated and the door open so that one day, when those in the dark decide to find their "I am" again, we will be ready.

To those of you who have chosen light at every juncture, we hug you and celebrate you. The few illuminate the way for the many. A single candle in a dark room lights the entire room. That is why we hold your hands and keep reminding you that you are loved. You, the warriors of light, are in the forefront of a wave that one day will reach everyone. We congratulate you for following your heart. We wish you to know that there is no substitute for truth and love. You are the great "I am" and the only one you must answer to regarding your choices. We ask you to consult your heart for each choice you make, and so be it.

The Game of Your Life

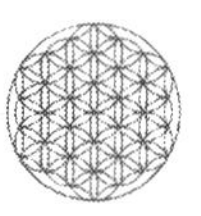

The beauty that you observe around you always reflects your inner landscape.

What about the ugliness, you ask?

That also, we say with a smile.

When you walk in the street and see an overflowing garbage bin, you may call it ugly. Another who walks the same street and looks at the same bin, may see it as a treasure, yet another who is an artist, may see it as beauty. Anything that streams in and out of your awareness is but an interpretation, a translation, of what you call reality. There is no such thing as an objective reality. There is actually no reality but your reality, which often is a fundamentally different reality than the one perceived by another standing beside you.

Why are you speaking about reality? We already know these things.

What you believe you already know, you do not. We speak about reality because you believe that you are one thing, yet you are not. You believe you already know who you are, who we are; what this universe is about, yet you don't. If a grain of sand was conscious and it could perceive the world from the vantage point of a grain of sand on the beach would you consider this vantage point an objective reality?

Would you consider the grain of sand immersed deep in the Atlantic Ocean to have the "true" vantage point of reality or the sand on a dune somewhere in the Sahara Desert? If your world were a grain of sand amidst as many grains of sand as you have in all your oceans and deserts combined, would you consider your grain of sand to have access to "true" reality? We can say with an absolute certainty that beauty is the essence of your true reality. But what is beauty?

Beauty is order, beauty is synergy, beauty is synchronicity; beauty is the pattern which guides all particles according to universal laws. The only reality that may be accessible to you, as you view the cosmos from the vantage point of a grain of sand, is a law that binds all grains to act in a similar fashion. (The law of gravity, for example.) The things that are invisible to you are not part of your reality, but the general cosmic laws you do observe are consistent, when they apply to all grains of sand everywhere. You are a galactic being and many of you have experienced conscious life, as you call it, while on other systems, beside this planet. Some have flashes of memory of a watery planet, or a fiery planet, some have flashed on a spidery planet or an underground existence planet. The cosmos is so vast and beyond the capacity of the human mind to fathom. Less so, does the human mind have the capacity to directly experience the multi-dimensional "reality" which is layered all around it. You have agreed to enter a reality that is limited in scope, so you could play.

Why play? You ask.

This is why you came here. You take your life so seriously that we must give you a little reminder of why you are here and the larger scope of your playing field. You come here to play, and before you enter this playing field, you set up for yourself the ground rules, you plan moves, and you strategize so you can play a "good" game. But often, as you play the game, you forget that it is just a game and you lose sight of why you came here to begin with.

You come to play. We ask you, then, to enjoy the game, do your best and know with full certainty, that what you call your reality is not. What you think this life is about it is not, either. The only truth that you can accept with no reservations is that you are a player and this is a game. So, enjoy the game. In this game, the most important thing is to play, as there are no winners and no losers. There are players and benchers. Many benchers wish to play and wait on the sidelines until one of the players moves aside and makes space for another to get off the bench and play. Never lose sight of the fact that you are only as good as you are true to yourself. What happens to those who forget that this is just a game? They begin to identify fully with their desires, their ambitions, and their idea of success; yet the real reason they came here is to play themselves, to play out their truth, their unique story, their purpose.

How many are in a forgetful place at this very moment, you ask?

Most, we say, but many are awakening and many more are being awakened.

Everything around you is an extension of your consciousness. The good, the bad, the beauty, the ugliness, the pain, the suffering, joy, and happiness. It is all there for you to choose from. It is on you to navigate the terrain and recreate the landscape that is inside of you and manifest it. Yes, it is true that not everything will go your way, but, what is your way? You want, wish, and desire certain things yet you may experience lack, hurt, anguish, pain, and suffering. Most of you want to have none of these elements in your life, but you also understand that there is treasure often cloaked in challenges and difficulties. You are master artists; you create the holographic landscape of your choice. Your power is limitless and you have no boundaries, but the one your own self creates. It is on you to break the perceived notion of a fixed reality and take flight.

Why should I bother, you ask?

The game you came to play has rules and unless you understand the rules of the game, and the game's purpose, you are just running around the playing field confused, baffled, and often in despair. Knowing what your journey is about, and the purpose of this game, can support you in taking flight.

Those of you on the path of awakening to your own truth, slowly peel away the layers, which mask the rules of this game. You understand that it is not about wealth or power, or even about happiness and joy. These are all reward points that can make life more comfortable, maybe enjoyable, and, while it is true that the better you learn to play, the easier it is to obtain and attract elements that make this game a true ecstasy, again, this is not what the game is about. Many believe that bliss, happiness, and joy are the ultimate goals. With a smile we say, yet again, it is not. If that were the case you would not have chosen this "school." There are plenty of others in the universe, where true bliss is just the starting point. And you go higher from there.

That is not the case here. With a universe so vast, do you truly believe that there are no other choices than to arrive at this sacred school you call Earth? You came here to play, to challenge yourself, to have the field open, so you may truly participate in the game of creation. Choices are the core element of this game.

In this vast infinite playing field, there are no goals, only markers. There are no wins, just moves which take you farther or send you backwards. There is nothing ultimate, or finite; just a continuum, a flow, a stream, a river that is endless with no beginning and no end. You float along and as you advance, you get closer to the ocean and when you reach the ocean, becoming one with the infinite body of water, you recycle, by evaporating and coming back as a raindrop, finding your way back to the river and again to the ocean. Each time you go through this cycle, you collect new experiences, like water absorbs minerals and sediments as it flows through bedrock and different terrains. Like that water, each experience enriches your spectrum and you then become the sustenance for all life around you. You become the engine of consciousness. If it was only about purity, you would not support life. The sediments you absorb, along the terrain of your journey, enrich the vibrational composition and mineral content so you can support all life. If happiness were the ultimate goal, why would you even come to this planet? If abundance were the ultimate goal, why, again, would you choose Earth? You are never forced to go to this school, yet many wait in line to make this pilgrimage so they can have an opportunity to play the game.

So play hard, play soft, play with your heart. Play love, play with courage; play with joy. Play happy; yet, know that this is just a game. In this game you lose by not playing and you win simply by playing.

Never lose sight of who you are. All our messages are like signs, markings, streetlights, guiding you how to play the game.

Can you give us the ultimate advice on how to play, you ask?

Use your heart, we say as we hug you. Through your heart you link to the vastness of the universal melody that makes the fabric of the playing field. You do not get lost when you use your heart. You elevate each experience to its highest degree when you use your heart. Being in the heart is being in the core of yourself. Whatever adventure you choose to experience, your heart is your most trusted navigator. In the game of creation there are many players, mostly invisible. The spectrum that you are able to perceive is so limited, that those who rely on the perceived reality to navigate, often make turns taking them farther away from their desired goals. It is the way of it. Your mind is programmed to act and react based on perceived reality. To play the game, you must learn not to rely solely on your perceived reality as you are limiting your ability to recreate it, change it, and transform it to serve you and others.

How, some ask?

Do not buy into it, know that it is all-relative. As the creator if you "buy" into any set of fixed rules, you make it more difficult to play. As a player, all options must remain open whether they are linear, circular, or multi-dimensional.

How do we start, you ask?

You dissolve the fixed rules residing within you, stating clearly that you have the ultimate authority over your own reality. Your reality is your kingdom and you can change the rules anytime you please. Not accepting the reality gifted to you by others is the crucial first step to becoming the co-creator and a true player. Everything in your environment since birth is there to create an illusion of a fixed reality with a set of unchangeable truths. From childhood, all the way to adulthood, you are being programmed to believe that the universe operates in a certain way and you must abide by certain truths to be able to navigate your life in a "successful way."

This must be dissolved. It is not an easy task, but it is the most essential aspect to becoming free. Being free is mostly about releasing fear, as fear is the most limiting programming of all.

Your goal is to open the playing field and make it a vast, limitless arena where everything is possible.

Being free of programs is where the game becomes interesting. The freer you become, the more immediate your reality transforms in response to your thoughts, feelings, and, yes, actions. However, the freer you are, the subtler the physical actions become, as matter responds to thoughts, emotions, and intentions as if there was a physical action.

Become free, play, do not wait, do not hold back, use your heart and release fear, clear your programming and know that your reality is reflected to you from the vantage point of one grain of sand, somewhere on a dune in the desert or a beach; it is just one grain of sand among all the grains of sand which represent different worlds and different realities that are available to you. Walk on the beach and scoop the sand into your hand. Let it then silently find its way back to the ground. Look at one of these grains of sand and know that this is your planet, this is Earth; lift your gaze upward. Breathe this vastness into you. You are a player and your playing field is infinite. Embrace that playing field and allow it to open fully, so you can have the game of your life, playing your true self, and so be it.

The Endgame

Play me a melody and I will dance to its rhythm, we say; universal law reads: *Ask and you shall receive*. We also say, *Do not ask and you shall receive, as well.*

How you ask and what you ask for is your melody. Just be, and all aligns. The sound you emit tells your story. Dance to your own melody and the cosmos will join you. Each of you comes with a mission, a purpose, a gift, in the form of a song. No song is more beautiful than the next. Each song is unique. The whole is not complete without even one of the songs remaining to be unsung. Within your world you assign value to yourselves. In the realm of the great "I am" there are no values assigned and no hierarchies. You measure your own self on how true you sing your song. Your gift is unique, not assignable, not exchangeable, not replaceable—like a puzzle being incomplete when even one piece is missing, regardless of whether this piece represents the sky or the eye of a Bambi.

What happens when I have found my song, you ask?

Some call it ascension. You have aligned with your purpose for coming and you have ascended to your next level without needing to shed your body. When a purpose is fulfilled, your journey continues to spiral up to your next journey. Your song, your gift, is deposited in the heart of the Earth and recorded in the library of records. Your journey never ends, so it is not about finishing anything. You came to gift all with your unique song.

The quality of your journey is a matter of personal taste. At the edge, is where all movement happens. In the center, there is silence. Intend to be on the fringes and you experience dramatic movement.

Intend to be in the center and all is still. Do you know where you wish to be? Is it the fringes or is it, the center?

Do you know what it is that you are searching for? Do you know who you are? Do you understand why you do the things you do? What motivates you to get up in the morning? Why is it that some of you are not feeling happy, or fulfilled, or joyful, while believing that you should? Do you have any idea why the world you occupy seems, at times, to be sliding backwards?

Ideas, so dark, that ought to have been abolished from your "now" are back in full swing; prejudices and hatred still prevail; poverty is still rampant, even while there is more than enough for every person on your planet, and then some. Why is it so? Why is there so much injustice built into your justice system? Why are poisons served in your food, corruption abounding in your health care systems, disparity in your social systems, insatiable greed, fueling economies based on lack and leading you to more disparity? Do you know? Do you have any clues as to the why of it?

What if we had told you that you have chosen every bit of it and that it is your melody to which reality, as you call it, is dancing? Do you truly believe that anything can take place without your permission? The day your collective decides to abolish anything, it will be gone forever. The day your collective will say no to greed, hatred, bigotry, abuse, exploitation, or violence, these expressions will be gone, never to return. Why do these things flower, then? The answer is as clear as the sight of a cloudless sky or the view of a freshwater stream on a sunny day: you, collectively, choose it to be that way, at any given day, hour, or moment. Breath by breath, heartbeat by heartbeat, you choose the reality in which you live.

Each thought, each action gets tallied and its collective flow steers the boat, directing the sails, and navigating the ship you call planet Earth. You have been given a playground, sacred and precious, which supports you in every which way. You are asked to play. Yet many of you are fast asleep. The sails are taking you somewhere and you are the passive passenger helping to move the boat, except that you have no idea where it is going. You are rowing while asleep and hoping for the best: for yourself, your children, and your children's children. If there were someone evil at one side and good at the other you would be able to excuse yourself, by saying, "I tried, but the other side, the evil, was too strong."

This reasoning is just an excuse, simply because it is not how things work. It is the responsibility of the few who are awakened, in each shift, to steer the boat safely. A cruise ship has a steering crew and a captain. It is not on the passengers to steer the boat; they rely on a navigator, the captain and its crew. Each passenger choses this journey by boarding the boat based on its destination. Your collective is mostly being led. Those who steer the boat safely are the ones who are aware of whom they are, who are awakened to their power, understand their responsibility, and vibrate in alignment with their truth. How do you change things when there are immense incoherent unconsciousness powers, in the midst of this game, with vast resources pulling to one side?

What is the endgame? you wish to know.

You stop playing their game, is our answer. As long as you play it, you cannot neutralize it or change it.

The endgame cannot be determined by a tug of war with powers, each pulling on opposite sides. This form of reality-making is messy, dualistic at its core, and does not recognize the divinity and choice, each has, to birth their own vision. Systems are based upon groups, which agree to certain rules. No system can survive without willing participants, not even for a day. The willing participants agree to accept a certain reality. Like, in language, when all agree that the letter A is the first and the letter Z in the last, as it is, in English. All agree that apple is a fruit. How do you, then, create any profound change that will end one game and begin a new one? Fight with these powers, under their own terms, and you push against forces that are too powerful. Direct confrontation often fuels these forces giving them even more combustive power.

How then, how does the endgame work? Very simply, it appears, from this side of the veil, that, from the moment you have awakened to the moments you go to sleep, you watch where your attention goes; how it is being directed. Watch the parts of you which are serving your "I am" and the parts; which are on autopilot, following the winds. Once you have been able to identify the parts of you that serve the "I am" and distinguish them from the parts of you that are being steered, then, slowly, you begin to shift your attention to where it serves the will of the "I am," that aspect of God within you. Doing so, inevitably, aligns you with your song and power. Mastery becomes fully engaged, in service to your own song; awakened and free. As you claim your mastery over your day, today, you advance to the crew, which navigate the ship, and you create a change. This is a large cruise ship, so that it changes course slowly.

Why is mastery so essential at this time? When you fully engage in the game and you understand your role, either at the center or at the fringes, you affect reality through your own being-ness.

Using the supermarket metaphor may help to emphasize our point.

In any basket that you take to the supermarket, there is a limit. Some baskets are small, some are big, but at some point—when you have filled the basket—it will overflow, as it reaches its capacity. As you walk the aisles, collecting items, your basket naturally becomes heavier and heavier and the things you collect become who you are. You can either ingest them, wear them, or decorate with them, using your selection to create the self. This supermarket represents what is available to you. The basket is where your attention goes, your energy, your light, your focus, your heart, your power.

What if you never enter the supermarket? You begin by removing each item you find in the basket, and make sure your basket remains empty. Your awareness and your attention remain a clear container and, each time something does fill it, you become aware of it, and use your power to deal with it, freeing yourself and clearing it away.

Your attention manifests your reality. The endgame is to watch it, direct it, and to be in control of it to such an extent that you become the captain of your ship, a master. When you are directing your own journey, you offer an alternative route to that cruise ship. You become a navigator by being the lighthouse for the ship.

If only a small fraction of you will reclaim your light, your reality, as you know it, will shift. The shift is not in your external actions, but in the quality of your song. Your being-ness is your melody. When you align with your melody, all particles must align around you rippling outward to all.

Why do we care? Why should we engage with the world, when all of it is made up of choices and all choices are honored? Why should we bother?

Because this is your song; this is why you came here and everything else will feel misaligned. When you engage with your world and you sing your song, you become it, and so be it.

What If?

As a human, you are an energy floating in space. The particles that surround you respond to your energy and are being continually reconfigured. From our perspective, you are a conscious nucleus of creative energy, directed to wherever your attention moves.

Your body is like a space station. It floats in space, and moves according to the gravitational forces surrounding it. Your own source of energy acts like a booster system, maneuvering and responding to those forces. In a cycle beginning with birth and continuing on, up through rebirth, you negotiate and navigate with the forces that surround you. The freer you become, the less effective those forces become at influencing your magnetic field. On a clear night, looking up, you observe the darkness of the sky. It appears, from your vantage point, that the celestial bodies are moving slowly in a predictable course, yet, if you take "time" out of the equation and see this movement from our perspective, celestial bodies, such as yourself, are in constant negotiation in regards to their gravitational field and, as the saying goes: "as above, so below." Every second of every minute of every hour of every day, these forces are in play. You are in play. When you emerge from the birth canal and begin your physical journey, you are fully aware of these forces. You can see them, hear them, feel them, and even taste them. As the circle settles into becoming a square and later shifts into a line, your ability to perceive forces, portals, and the magic that surrounds you, slowly diminishes, while your linear perceptions become more acute. As you probably guessed, some of you are still partially linked to the circle, and as a result their ability to communicate "normally" is somewhat limited. There are those who, more easily, maintain part of their awareness in the circle. Your establishment has tagged many of them, as "autistic" or "challenged," with diminished capabilities to express and communicate "normally." Many whom you may consider handicapped, are, from our perspective, enhanced light beings, more readied to absorb and exist in multi-dimensional reality. In the not too distant future, it will become transparent why. These abilities, to be partially linked to the circle while occupying a physical body, represent an evolutionary leap. Currently you consider it a problem, and attempt to medicate, manipulate, or teach these light beings, the carriers of this enhancement, so they can become like you; "normal."This approach is about to change and, in time, will be reversed. You will grow to perceive linearity as limiting. It is "the linear" ones who will need special teaching and adaptation while the "abnormal ones" will become the adepts. You are rapidly expanding into a multi-dimensional field; still there are many who resist "seeing" it (and acting according to its influences). The Mayan, Incas, Egyptians, and further back, the Atlanteans and the Lemurians, were far more aligned with the cosmic forces. In your distant history a shift occurred in balance when the masculine linear mental field became dominate and as a result overshadowed the feminine cyclical field, causing you to become increasingly adrift, trapped by this mental cage. This mental field is currently out of balance with Earth's equilibrium. You, having come full circle, are now having these abilities reintroduced to you through your children. Many of them choose to emerge with this upgrade despite the discomfort involved.

For the good news, we say with a smile; feminine portals worldwide are awakening and beginning to pulse again rippling, weaving, introducing heart-based melodies. The feminine must reclaim its place and move back into power to correct the misalignment. Sacred it is.

You have a responsibility; a mission of sort and it has to do with you and you only. When there is a desire to find your light, it is always followed by a yearning to uncover the truth. Truth has no perspective; it's devoid of interpretation. Truth stares at you, as you stand naked: self-evident, apparent, and as transparent as a clear sky.

When you face truth, it is not followed by a need to act, but by a desire to accept, a surrendering of sorts, a melding of the various aspects of the one into a larger "I am" that represents your light. If you were told that your world was coming to an end would you do anything different? Would you hug more? Forgive more? Love more? Relax more? If you were told that, at the end of this day, you are going to be finished here, would you live the seconds, moments, or hours you have left differently than you would have if that information was not available? Would you choose to watch TV if you knew that the clock is ticking and you are but minutes away from an enormous shift changing all that you have ever known? You are a visitor, a tourist, an alien, and an outsider, who, just for a moment, has an opportunity to play. This game that you play is for real, yet it is just a game. Your experiences are real, yet they are real only when you are playing your part in the game. Once the game ends, all that you have experienced becomes, yet another movie. So what would you choose today if you knew that the end of the game draws near? Would you choose to travel more, to laugh more? Would you remain just where you are?

The world is not ending anytime soon and your journey will not end anytime soon. We do ask, though, that you peer into the "what if" and feel where it takes you. From our perch, every moment counts, and yet, time is meaningless. When you count time, you act like time is everything, but where we come from, space devoid of time, your thoughts, feelings, and actions define you. The way you think affects the way you feel and the way you act. It becomes who you are. Your uniqueness is your gift. Your gift is your uniqueness. Search for it, clear all that is not you, the time is now. So much of whom you believe you are is gifted to you. Now, it is time for gifting you with yourself.

How would we know our true self from our false self, you ask?

Your false self involves fear of one type or another; truth always involves love, devoid of fear. See to it that the invisible golden strings of love whisk you higher when you become agitated or confused. Wrap yourself in a shield that is sewn by a magical seamstress and know that you are where you need to be.

We are you and you are us. Merging with us is merging with God. Merging with another human is merging with God. When two have become one, the one becomes the whole. Each of you carry the spark, the potential, to become one with the whole. Most of you discover your own divinity through merging with another human. In the moment of entering another body, this is where your soul has the potential to be touched, the deepest. You call it love, you can call it sex. It is a profound experience for a human angel that has the power to birth immense light as well as immense darkness. A body is a nucleus held together by magnetics and by intention. When one nucleus merges with another, a reaction takes place. This reaction carries with it, the potential of immense release. And, it is why this aspect of divinity was excluded from all religions, kept subjugated, was persecuted, manipulated, laid bare to charges of corruption while, at the same time, seemingly abhorred.

Like water, your natural state is cyclical. Your awareness and your body must come alive, must be brought online, and activated, in order to be able to safely contain the higher frequency of your ever-shifting cosmic environment. The new children, that generation of children you may have sometimes tagged "autistic," will also be the generation who must undo the chains keeping your sexual energy behind bars. This energy must remain free of any hooks. Freedom is circular. There is no hierarchy. The womb, with its yoni, the planet, your sun, and your light are all-spherical in their essence. The dimension of spirit is always spherical. Most of you live within lines, which begin and end at particular points in space. It is on you to curve those linear edges, reconnecting the beginnings and endings of these lines; once again building up your awareness that you are constantly forming and moderating circles (and your cycles, as well). We are only asking you to listen and to become attuned to the whispers all around you. Understand that each moment awakened is a meditation where reality is creating from within, manifesting outwardly. When you are "asleep" the gravitational forces all around you dictate your outer manifestations. When you exchange energy with another human via speaking, listening, hugging, merging, or even dreaming, acknowledge the sacredness of the exchange and honor it as a meditation. When you awake, your inner vision will be open, all exchanges become significant, each spark of energy you emit to another human changes you, as well as the other. When you make love to another, you make love to yourself. The feeling, sensation, and pleasure is within you. Honor it as meditation. When you begin to see every moment as this meditation, the universe will reflect back to you precisely the state you reflect to the universe, a reflection of sacredness and love. When you meditate for ten minutes a day and then, the rest of the day, you spend in a state of "sleep," it is as if you took a pain relief pill while continuing, simultaneously, to make your pain worse.

Each act is a meditation and the most revered meditation is when you enter another person or another person enters you through love. The shrine, the holy of holies, is within you. To neutralize the corruptive, incoherent melodies of the past, honor each exchange with another human as you would honor an exchange with God, him, and herself. Know that the sphere is always there. Know that the realities you are opening, as well as yourself, have always been around. It is your time to awaken to the larger sphere around you and to become activated, so you can easily contain that larger you, awakening and accepting this expanding story, and so be it.

The Gate

We love you and we wish you to wake up to your melody, not for our sake, but for your own. Sleeping offers many advantages, none of which align with your reason for coming here. Anytime you create a ripple of energy from your core you illuminate your field. When your field is illuminated, even for a split second, your environment is transformed from dark to light and those who are lost can see, if only for that split second, where they are, and may change direction. Imagine a young woman walking in complete darkness. Slowly she has stretched out her hands and her eyes are wide open, but she can see nothing. Hesitantly she keeps advancing toward an unknown destination, hoping for the best, but fearing the worst. Then, as if from nowhere, a flash of light illuminates the environment and she manages to see, in that split second, the edge of the cliff, right in front of her, which would likely have brought her demise. At that moment she changes course 180 degrees and walks the opposite way, away from danger, away from the cliff, away from her demise, and into a new future. If you knew that, each time you ripple, that it changes someone else's life, then would you be more committed? Trust that your ripple makes a difference and changes lives. We ripple all the time, but in a frequency that is not easily perceived or felt by human angels. Your ripple, however, does transform lives. For each ripple there is a name attached, a story, a life. For each open heart, there are ten which are closed. For each ray of light, there are nine dark corners waiting to be illuminated, transformed, exposed. The comfort of darkness allows you to act without awareness of the consequences of your actions.

We know who you are. We know your past. We know your present and we see all your potentials. It is our job to know and it is your job to trust. If you knew what we know, the place you call home would not serve its purpose. It would not give you a fertile ground to grow. Many of you wish to know what to do and where to go to reach that place of bliss, joy, happiness, and illumination. We can tell you where this place is, right where you are, and all of you know it. Each twenty-four hours gives you a gate to walk through. Each hour is a potential for opening. We do not count time in seconds or minutes, but in the gates you walk through. If you had not walked through any gates in a cycle, time stood still. You stayed a young soul. Most of the planet is in the toddler to young soul state and it is an exciting action-based reality. Those of you in the mature range perceive reality very differently, as most of the action carrying any weight takes place inside of you. What happens outside is used as a context, a backdrop, a set design for the internal play. The subtler your field becomes, the more your internal and external realities align. What you believe in, think about, and feel in your heart, reflects who you are and how your life unfolds. Each sunrise offers opportunities to make choices. These choices open gates and create movements. Some are conditioned to ignore the gates and move by as if they are not there. Some slow down and celebrate each gate appearance, align to it with gratitude and walk through. Know that a gate appears only when you are ready to open it. If you missed one, another will show up to replace it. There is no loss. You are eternal. One lifetime is replaced with another and gates appear each time, when you are ready. It is on you, and you only, to trust, knowing when to open a gate, then, again, to trust when to walk through. When you walk through a gate, it always involves resistance, so expect it, honor it, and celebrate. Walking through gates requires conquering fear, very real, existential fear, fear of death. Expect it, celebrate it, honor it, and congratulate yourself while walking with eyes open. If it did not involve fear it would not be a gate. Walking from one field of vibration to another requires courage, trust, surrender, perseverance, persistence, humility, and authenticity.

Why fear of death you ask?

You walk into the unknown, the abyss, the void, and only when you have walked through the portal can you see again, although never in the same way. Your vision changes, your perception changes, and your interpretations change. You enter one and exit another. Like death, you walk into the unknown and no matter how many would promise you that death is but a gate, you still experience fear, existential fear. It is your journey and you designed it that way.

What happens to those who walk life after life, without opening any gates, you ask?

They are as sacred as those who walk through many gates. You are to honor them, as one day they will open their eyes and take a leap. Maybe they will see where they are because of the ripple you have created. Do not confuse spiritual work with walking through gates. Mastering the spiritual arena is like a map, as it helps you see where you are at the moment. All human angels are spiritual. All have the capacity to create light. All, also, have the ability to choose. Some walk the path that is deemed spiritual and some walk a path that is deemed material. Using spiritual knowledge of the past does not guarantee you access. Knowing the spiritual language, terminology and using it appropriately, does not buy you entry tickets. Your spiritual practices are but tools. Many confuse spiritual practice with being spiritual. It is as if a dog is only a dog if it barks. You are all spiritual, and you all have access to spiritual wisdom and practices, none of which guarantees you a key to a gate. Gates are often messy, chaotic, scary, confusing, and challenging to the core, asking you to walk on the cliff's edge while closing your eyes. Walking through a gate in one's lifetime is a cause for celebration. It is as if you were to walk on a tightrope, balancing the impossible and holding yourself in light. It does not matter if you have studied all the spiritual wisdom available and you know it by heart, when a gate appears on your path, you will be challenged. It is the way of it. You can be a revered Lama in some Tibetan monastery, an honorable Bishop, a mechanic who fixes cars, or a goat herder in some remote land, when your gate appears, it will be challenging.

Why would I walk through a gate if it were so horrible and unpleasant, and I surely do not wish to die?

We did not say it is horrible and unpleasant, and you do not die, you just feel as if you are dying. Walking through a gate is scary, challenging and a life changer.

Many of you walk only when you must and you all know which gate you are forced to walk through, the ultimate one. The one at the end of your cycle. Moving from one level of vibration to another requires you to move through a gate. However you choose to interpret the portal, it will take you to higher ground, allowing you an opportunity to broaden your playing field, and will move you into a more expansive cosmic arena. Wouldn't you want to explore the limits of your being? What can be more sacred than moving beyond the boundaries of time, space, and matter, merging with the totality of existence? Our promise to you is that, once you have emerged on the other side of a gate and look, the most common whispers we hear are: What a blessing! What took me so long? Why was I so scared?

All of you must move through at least two gates in a cycle, the gate of birth and the gate of what you consider physical death. Any consequent gate may feel like both death and re-birth. When you move through a gate you must leave something behind that may not cross with you, and you give birth to an aspect of your expanded "I am" that you could not access before. Gates appear before you when you are ready and you do not need to intend for it, only identify and know when they show up.

So what does love has to do with those gates?

We thought you would never ask, we say with smile.

Gates open through love and to cross to the other side you must be love. No other ingredient will work. It must be a purely authentic and transforming melody. The melody of love opens the key to a gate and the gate's frequency guides you through a seemingly impossible maze to emerge reborn. Using any other melody would get you more lost. Again, it is the way of it. You are a human angel in a school of free choice. That choice is yours, and so be it.

Darkness

We are back, and you are too. We are pleased that you keep showing up on time, to once again allow us to come through.

What is it that separates a human from an angel? What separates one human from another? What causes a newborn child, who emerges with no prejudices, to begin a separation process? When and how do you learn to hate one another? How and when do you learn to un-love one another? Where is the place inside of you, which through alchemy, becomes tainted and spoiled? Why do souls come here to experience a separation from oneness? What are the mechanics of spirit discombobulating, disintegrating, deconstructing, and destroying, as the separation takes place, leaving behind its original state of purity and love? How does spirit fall from grace into the abyss, to the void, and into the depths of darkness? Why do human angels end up evil, anti-spiritual and inhuman?

This is one long question, you may complain. Indeed, and a question that humanity has been grappling with for eons.

What if we told you that this is one of the reasons souls come to this sphere of reality, to this planet? What if we told you that darkness is precisely the magnet that makes this sphere of free choice, a prime real estate, in a large cosmos?

The natural state of souls in this infinite arena of a cosmos is light and love. Earth is the exception, not the rule.

What if we told you that darkness is inbuilt to your reality and is embedded in the cosmic laws that govern your sphere? This, in turn, maintains your Earth as, a unique vibrational experience. Souls in this vast universe, who do incarnate, rarely encounter darkness, sometimes never. It is not a natural state of being, for a spirit to experience.

What if we told you that, in this reality, it is precisely the thing you hate, the thing you complain about so much, that is also the precise reason you are here? To live through it, to know it, to make peace with it, to learn to transmute it, to transform it, and to know that darkness and light are states of being, intimately connected. You came here to expand your idea of the shadow, to look at the range of grays and to review any idea you had about the spectrum, maybe even to suspend judgment about the dark, and to suspend judgment about the light.

What if you were told that those who you consider the most sinister and insidious in your culture, as well as in your history, volunteered, willingly, to play their part, just like you volunteered to play your part, as a lighthouse?

What if we had taken you to a large theatre and opened the closed curtain, the veil some call it, just a crack, so you could have a peek at some of the rehearsals and of the preparations taking place in the between life theatre, prior to the process of descent into what you call your reality?

What would I see behind that veil, you may ask?

Enemies rehearsing lines, feuds being planned, atrocities being choreographed, volunteers being called to choose which one they will participate in, and what would take place to serve their growth and evolution.

There are neither children, nor adults, nor women, nor men, there are only light beings, some call them angels, who have signed up to experience duality, to undergo separation, to learn about the emotion of hate, to see violence with their own eyes, maybe even their bodies. Some wish to know for the first time what physical death feels like, what pain feels like, how hunger, thirst, deprivation, anger, rage, fear, anxiety, or panic feel, and how to then emerge on the other side stronger, expanded, more confident, grateful, and ultimately find love again; that of self which extends to others.

Why would they ever wish to do so? It's crazy to actually want to go to a place of lack, of darkness, of pain, from a place of infinite light and love.

When you are light, when you are a soul, when you are an angel, learning and growing on the other side of the veil, your perspective is somewhat different.

Your priorities are guided by your vibration expanding. This expansion is fueled, if you will, by the range of experiences you collect along your journey.

Let us say that you are floating in light, surrounded by cotton balls, for a hundred thousand human years, watching, from above, all that is transpiring on Earth: all the exciting moments, the entire range of emotions, the craziness of conflicts, the prospects of winning or losing, the tasks of overcoming adversities, moving through insurmountable obstacles, physical, mental, or emotional, yet to emerge victorious. So you watch all that from the comfort of your angelic living room, sipping angelic nectar. At some point, even, you may wish to, at least once, for just a while, experience some action, becoming one of the actors in the illusion you call your reality.

There are billions of angels like you, who are standing in long lines to come to where you are now. We say, not millions, but billions, and why is it so? This school is unique, because it allows darkness and light to battle each other from a place of free choice.

For this school to offer the range and richness it was designed to give, darkness must play a part, and it always will, on some level.

What do you mean some level? Does it ever change for the better?

The short answer is yes. The long answer is yes but…

You have chosen, as a collective, to ascend from your current level to a higher vibration, on a subtler level of being.

Everyone ever incarnated on Earth, or to be incarnated, was present at that meeting where you, as a collective (some call this collective "God"), chose to keep going, but differently than ever before. Your choice was creating an immense ripple movement in the cosmos. You had a deadline to cease, to reboot (something that happened many times before) and you chose to go on. That is extremely rare, it created a media buzz, and flashed into the headlines of the galactic news broadcast and beyond.

The choice was made by your collective, announced by celestial synchronized alignments sometimes named the Harmonic convergence in August 1987, twenty-nine years to the day this message was given to you, anchored by the delivery of feminine activation marked by the Venus transit event twenty-five years later on June 6th, 2012. With these events and your collective choice, the rules of the game have changed.

The rules of free choice remained intact, but many of you asked for this school to become of the light. As darkness is an integral aspect of this school, internal conflict emerged where all were asked to make a choice. That choice was presented with a deadline at the end of the calendar year of 2012.

This is a greatly simplified short version of a very interesting dramatic shift in your collective evolution.

Once the new trajectory was created, no one, not even those who voted for it and designed it, had any idea or control of where it was going. You wiped your trajectory clean and moved on to a clean slate where you guide the direction, speed, intensity, and outcome of your next chapter.

It moved from the known to the unknown; from a predicted outcome to a complete mystery. You have collectively garnered sufficient power to chart your own path and it is anyone's guess as to where it is leading. You have taken your power back, which changes your course, so now it is up to you and you only, at this point of your evolution, to choose what kind of school the precious place you call home will be: of the light or of darkness. You have representatives from both sides battling each other. You have asked it to be of light, but there are no guarantees that your request will be granted. There are angels, just like you, who wish to see it remain just as it has been.

It is awe-inspiring, to many around you, that you were able to surpass the expectation of everyone that was watching. All bets were on you not succeeding, yet you have taken back a power that was not in your possession from the beginning of your journey, not a small feat. You have taken back the power to chart your own path.

We are of the light, we are your guides, as we are an aspect of your expanded "I am." We hold no judgment of the dark but it is not our vibration. We love you and we support you if you wish to take back your power to bring light to the darkest corners of this school of free choice.

Your playing field offers you now a true choice and you are leading the way. Immense light is being created, but the dark mounts its own campaign. Your work is not yet finished, no, it has actually just begun, and know that, for this work, your heart is your most powerful tool.

Those who chose dark, volunteered to be your teachers, so that you have known what to expect. You have watched this place evolve over millennia. Know that those who chose to bring pain and suffering did so in agreement with those who suffer, but the rules have suddenly transformed and you have the power, now, to awaken to a reality that was once not available to you, on your channel list.

You came here for a reason. Your goal is to bring light to where there was none. You are loved and it is your time to fulfill the purpose you came here for, and so be it.

Happiness

Nowhere were you promised that your journey would be easy. You were promised that it would be interesting; that it is a worthwhile pilgrimage; that it will challenge you, and stretch your abilities; that it might frighten you, and be painful at times. You were shown all the gateways to open your heart, and find light in places where it is scarce, but at no time were you told that it would be a breeze, or that you came to this dimension to be happy.

Happiness, joy, or bliss is a byproduct and not a goal. Your soul does not aim to be happy, your soul aims to be truthful, to be awake, to seek, face, and challenge itself to grow, to learn, and eventually, to find peace, and ultimately love, for self. Nowhere in your soul blueprint and path, is it searching for happiness.

Yet, all you want for yourselves, your children, your loved ones, is for them to be happy.

How could it be, you ask, *that everyone wants something, that soul could not care less about? Are we all part of the same illusion*, you ask?

Indeed, you are. You have been "programmed" to be in a place of hope, rather than just be. As your ancestors were searching for the perfect ingredients to control you, to subdue you, to turn you into a malleable, pliable, gullible human, they have implanted concepts that will keep you away, from being exactly where you are now. You developed a keen ability to project, to hope, to have illusions, to have desires, wishes, and ambitions, all for something, happening in the future. Once you are anchored into the future, your power diminishes, and your ability to manifest, to create, and to perform your magic, is hindered. You are like a ship stranded and beached, unable to sail. Sailing means being fully present, while the desire for joy, happiness, and hope, are concepts that only suspend you, in the future.

Soul wishes to be free always, to roam the vast field of energy, and to explore. Human consciousness, on the other hand, in its current level of awakening, wishes to sooth fears and is predominantly guided by survival, and in order to reduce fear and survive, it uses methods of manipulation, controlling one another, as well as creating a false sense of security, through a continuing accumulation.

Those who are indeed happy are those who do not seek happiness; those who bathe in joy are those who do not go out trying to be joyful; and those who are in bliss are those who gave up on searching and are firmly anchored in just being.

There are those who wish everyone else to be subservient, acquiescent, submissive, yielding to them, very much like the slave owner and slave relationship. What those slave owners do not consider, is that when they attempt to hold anyone in bonds, they create bondage for themselves. One cannot ever be free, while holding others in bonds. The oppressor and the repressed are two ends of the same force, bringing together both sides in a dual match, and maintaining both, in chains. You cannot ever be free yourself, when you have others subservient to you. The dance of high and low, slave and owner, repressed or oppressed, are two sides of the same coin. Being free is the highest space your light wishes to occupy. It is your ultimate reason for being you. You come to free yourself from things: from people, from karma, from concepts, projections, or programming; from heaviness, and from the ideas of hope or happiness, joy, or bliss. Being free is, pure and simple, just being, exactly where you are at this moment, inhaling and exhaling, feeling the universal pulse echoing through your heart, and offering gratitude for your existence in this physical dimension. Although this "being" concept is rather simple, it eludes most, as the programming inserted into your collective reality, in the form of desire for happiness.

How can it be bad to hope for a better future? How can there be anything wrong with wanting to be happy, in joy or in bliss, you ask in frustration?

If you see what we see, you will know that each time you seek something in the future, at that very moment you project it into the future, the very thing you so desired becomes no longer available to you. Each time you desire what you do not have, you create a hologram of lack, and built around this hologram, is a desire to create even more lack.

Universal laws are dispassionate about your desires, your wishes, your fears, and your projections. They work, in a manner, that responds to all your mental chatter in the same, even, way. Every thought, every concept, that you ever held in your consciousness; every fear, every hope, they are all taken literally, and are being drawn into your master plan, your cosmology, your map. You project into the future, and the future brings you back the exact things you fear the most, as well as pushes away, the exact things you are desiring. The literal nature of these laws becomes translated into opposites. When you fear something, you actually attract it to your field, and when you crave or hope for something, the law keeps it as a hope and a desire, that never gets fulfilled. That is the way of it, in simplistic terms.

"The landlords" knew of the hermetic equations, and how the universe operates. They, then, invented hope, as a counter to a mind framed to being in the present. Hope is always a projection into the future, a desire for something that you currently do not possess. Hope was sold as a remedy for despair, so those who are currently in dark places, could find solace in something that might happen in the future. The "hope" concept, therefore, weakens those hopefuls, by moving him or her away from being powerful in the now, into a presence of weakness projected into the horizon.

What you are telling us is an outrage, some may cringe. *Without hope, we are doomed?*

Normally, at this point, we lift and hold you close to our angelic hearts so you can find comfort in the knowledge that truth is love.

Hope takes you away from your truth, to an abstract mental construct. That is weakness. To be in hope, is to be asleep, and that is what dooms you. To be in your power, you must align with your current reality construct, and, within that construct, be fully awakened and present. You bring yourself gradually to a new understanding of this construct, one that actually serves you, one that expresses love for self, one that has forgiveness and gratitude written into the notes of its melody. Being present, and altering your comprehension of your story in the now, changes your physical reality instantly. This is the way of it. Your prayers, therefore, weaken you, your wishes weaken you; your fears weaken you. Are you still surprised, when reality projected to you through your media seems so bleak, that all you have left is hope, which is an illusion, a mental construct devoid of power?

So, what happens, when you move from this mental construct, into your heart?

Everything!

Why so?

Your heart beats, and is always in the now. When you are residing in your heart, you are in the now, connected through invisible strings to you and to everything around you: to people, to animals, to flowers, to the elements, to the invisible world, and the cosmos, as well.

Any hopes, wishes, desires, fears, are all channeled through your mental construct, through your mind, and are never a product of the heart. The heart ripples in purity.

What we are sharing with you, is within the mystery of mysteries, of opposites. You are free, you are love; you are your heart, you are here as a right; you are here to add to the whole, you are here as a divine being; you are here as an angel with invisible wings; you are here to walk the path of trust, truth, love, and mastery over your own core power.

Holding on to this basic knowing, being awakened and present, neutralizes the mental construct and squares you with the central reason you are here. You came, to find you. But you cannot find you, in the mental field because it does not exist there. Your mental field is a decoy, an illusion, Maya. You can only find you, when you are aligned with you, in the presence of your wholesomeness and awake.

We ask you to awaken so you may find yourself, so you may link to your power, to your light, to the "I am."

When you are in your power, you carry sufficient energy to light up everything around you. When you walk illuminated, all those who cross your path asleep, now have an opportunity to awaken. Simply put, it is your choice, and that is why so many of you made the pilgrimage to this sacred, auspicious school you call Earth. And so be it.

The Trench

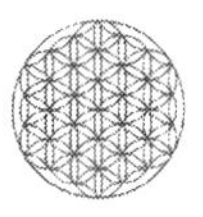

How do I begin, you ask? *Where do I find the thread? How do I know that this is, indeed, what I have been seeking?*

Your mind is working continually. Its job: creating thoughts, building up concepts, imagining things that have never existed before. It makes up stories. It names objects it sees. It remembers the past and projects into a future, where it creates fears and worries, hopes, dreams, and desires. Your mind naturally wishes to justify its own existence and perpetually spins a cocoon of all of these things around itself. If it ceases to create thoughts, it ceases existing. Your mind, from its inception, is on a struggle to survive. It never wants to stop its cycles of movements because, the day it stops, is the day you may discover that you manage quite well without it. Can you imagine moving about in your world having your mind set on suspension?

So how do you find the thread? Which thread are you looking for and how do you know when you have found it?

The simple answer is that you never really know.

The even simpler answer is that it does not really matter.

You place an enormous importance on the "what" and on the "why." What will I do with my life and why should I choose the sciences over medicine? Why should I go to this place, yet not to that place? More often than not, you are just edging closer to your comfort zone; to what you know. If your father was a policeman, you may end up some sort of policeman as well, because you are already familiar with what it represents, what it means, and how it feels. Many of you call it your destiny because it seems to fit like a glove to your circumstances. We call this your "trench." You slipped into the familiar trench. Once there, you may find that the walls of this trench grow taller and become even more slippery, creating a great challenge to any who may wish to climb out. Here is our question to you: Why is it mattering which thread you choose or where it leads you?

We see you from the perspective of the grand circle. Use your mind, for a moment, to imagine yourself as a dot at the center of a core, which is itself the center of a large sphere. Into one of your lifetimes the core center sends a thread in a direction that is called "the shoemaker." At another lifetime, the center draws a thread along a direction that is called "the judge." Another lifespan runs to a direction called "family man." Yet another goes to a direction called "the seamstress." You have had a thousand and one lives (actually many more), each one a thread, pointing to a different experience and still connecting back to the core. Those threads are what make you who you are. It is not the specific lifetime where you were more important, richer, or more accomplished, that matters. It is not the influence of your clout or your treasures that makes one lifetime more significant than another. You are a collective of all your lifespan experiences, from before anyone began to count time. We call it before the beginning. Some of you are ancient. The older you are within this never-ending cycle of death and rebirth, the less it matters what or why, and the more it matters how; how you move within the fields of energy, how you relate to yourself and others, within the context of your life, how you feel, how you honor, how you choose, how you do your dance, how enthusiastically you play your melody. You can be this or that; earn that much or be in great debt. You can be a single person or have a large family; the context that you are born into is just a starting point and it matters less than you might imagine. You are so much larger than any of you can really fathom. If you take a pencil and draw the largest circle you can on a piece of paper; then, in the center draw a point, that point is you, yet the circle is closer to the real you. Who you think you are is a dot and who you truly are is a transcendent glowing sphere.

Do not complain about the circumstances of your life or fret over the poor choices you have made. Just know that this moment is only the starting point and it matters little. The context is only the stage set in the theater. What is important, really important, is the acting or, even more than this, the character of the actor. How do you navigate the fields of energy all around you? How much love is being weaved into what you do? Within the circle there is no high or low. The sphere is void of hierarchies and before, or after, do not exist. The only thing that matters is your relationship to the core; the core being you and a vast, expansive, multi-dimensional, all encompassing "I am," the aspect of you that is God.

We say God, yet we refer to the self that is you, the collective you. Religions have weakened you by inserting the concept that there is a God outside yourself and that you somehow need to appease it. In fact, the opposite is the truth. You are it; you always have been, and will be. There is no one out there beside you and your role is to be aligning with the expanded you, merging with it, honoring and embracing it, and containing it. When you do that, life becomes an adventure since the powers unleashed when you merged with your "I am" are nothing short of miraculous.

So, what is keeping you from merging with yourself?

We can only guess, is it fear, cultural conditioning, or religion? Is it your unendingly busy mind? Yet, all these are but excuses; strategies for you to avoid yourself. And what is it that is behind the avoidance?

When you merge with the expanded "I am" you can never be a victim; there is no one to blame ever; you take responsibility for all that happens to you in your surroundings, in your world, and in your reality. This way is absolute. There is only you and your "free will" choices. Most of you find it more convenient to blame another, perhaps something that you cannot control, larger and more powerful than yourself, like a God, nature, politics, and those outside of you who pained you in some way and prevented you from being more fully you. We have also described this comfortable zone of submission as moving into the trench. Many of you are giving your powers to the highest bidder, may it be the head of the family, the spouse, the political power, or just circumstances. Once it is outside of you it does not matter, really, who you assign as the guardian of your power, what is important that it is not you.

What is the key, one may ask, *to re-merging and aligning with my power?*

We spoke about your mind, and how it loves to build concepts, to justify its existence. The mind is a construct you use to explain to yourself your present reality. Begin by suspending that power for a short while and see what happens. The mind creates concepts that have borders, conceptual lines, and parameters, so it can analyze itself, breaking down the reality around it for understanding; parsing that reality into parts and components, although the world is really not that way. You exist in a field that cannot be disseminated the way the mind does it. You can attempt it, but you will only create more confusion. You may understand parts of the whole, yet you will completely miss the grandeur of its wide-open scope.

So, what do we do? You insist.

You glide into your heart, and there you rest. Suspend any desire to think; just rest. The whole unravels slowly, allowing you to sense the real world. The whole cannot be perceived by the mind since the mind thinks only in limits. It created ways to measure because this is the way it is built. A bee sees pollen and ignores much of the rest since its survival depends on it. You create boundaries and borders because that allows your mind to justify its own existence. Your reality can only be sensed as a feeling, not as a mental construct. This is not new. You already know well this subject as many of you struggle, at this time, to merge with your own entirety.

So why do we repeat something that has been presented to you again and again, many times?

To remind you of your power. You are coming into a period where you may experience your reality as swirling fields of energy colliding, turning everything topsy-turvy along a natural path. From our perspective, this is a chaotic set design for any mind to fathom and contain; yet the heart remains un-phased. Trying to take in and digest your "now" reality can bring stress, worry, anxiety, fear, and despair. Your mind is trying to make sense of a portion of a reality it perceives. We ask you to step into the sphere and see it from our perch: All movement is correct, all actions are accurate, all represent a choice, and your reality is unveiling to you, based on your free will, in a linear time-space continuum.

The next time you feel despair, allow the larger you to take you on a journey outside the parameters of your mind, showing you all about this game, that you are the main player and it is time that any and all ideas of others be cleared from your repertoire. The game is you. It all starts with you and ends with you. When you choose, you create; when you create, the particles around you transform to allow the blueprint you have created to manifest.

So, what is this concept of the trench, some may wonder?

When you are born, your default path we call the "trench." It means that you are guided by the circumstances of your life and, just like water, you flow to where life leads you, so that you move down the path of your ancestors.

Some call it destiny or fate. We could call it the "zero-point," since this means you have not woken up. The first indication of one's awakening is getting out of the trench. You become the master of your life by beginning to understand that you create everything, all the time. Describing your lifetimes as destiny or fate is again another excuse.

So now, what is next?

Everyone in your close circle will fight you; your environment will resist your awakening, since the trench is so comfortable to everyone around you, no work is required; like water, you flow along to the lowest point guided by gravity.

Awakening is learning to use your multi-dimensional wings, which thrive when gravity and resistance are present, so you may take flight. The trench is your default path, the one that is set up for you, if you chose to keep on sleeping in a particular lifetime. Once awakened, the first call of the day is to climb up the slippery, tall walls of the trench and get out. This is the way it always works.

There is little movement when you are asleep. There is a celebration on our side as you begin to awaken. You are a dot in a vast sphere and the thread that you create within the sphere weaves the reality with which you may merge. It happens whether you are aware of it or not, but we ask you now, to weave consciously using your heart, and so be it.

Fulcrum

Despite all the love you give to the world, you still lack love for self, *how could that be,* you wonder? Wherever you turn there is no escaping self, yet most search for ways to not be present, and when you have found a path that is proven to sufficiently remove you from self you celebrate it by over-walking that path.

Why would you wish to escape self? The answer is simple, because it is easier than facing the self.

Many of your newly discovered spiritual schools teach you ways to escape. Very few teach you how to be present, and the reason is that it is hard. Facing, being present, seeing who you are is frightening to most. It is easier telling your self a story, using words that are comforting and painting a picture that mask how you truly feel about self. Self comes here to work, to clear, to dive deep, to die over and over, to transform, to transmute, to grow, to move into its truth, its core, to fully face itself, and it is not afraid of death. Often, however, it takes unimaginable forces to bring the self to finally meet self.

You much rather see yourself with make-up and costume, or use projections, and transference strategies to avoid seeing who you really are. All that you experience, the good, the bad, and the ugly, comes from you and no one else. This is not new to you.

This trajectory of moving away from self has been developed over thousands of years and now its core is melting together with the ice in your poles. It simply can no longer hold the limiting illusionary reality that you have created. Everything is changing, and when we say everything we mean everything, from the Earth resonance also known as the Schumann resonance, to weather patterns, your DNA, and the celestial forces operating around you. There are enormous galactic and planetary movements and you are placed at the center of it. Some indeed may hold on to the illusion that all it is the same, yet most sense deep inside that it is not.

In order for you to shift the energy field around you, you must be one with that field and in coherence, fully conscious, and awake. When you are removed from the alignment with your field, you are an easier target, your fulcrum is tilted to one side, and most of your energy is spent on just staying balanced.

What is it that is being asked from me now? You ask while we surround you with our wings, laying our heads in a circle to form a link to the greatness of this sphere of existence you occupy.

Know this; the answer is simple; nothing at all.

Contrary to a popular misconception, you did not come to do but to be. The oxymoron is that you may undo your self by doing too much. The possibility of your demise did not scare you from coming here, and at times, on the contrary, have encouraged many souls to take birth and try to change that which was a very real potential short time ago. We wish to share what is being asked from you outside the doing, and in the realm of the being.

Being is difficult, much more than you can imagine. It is the quintessential of any deep transformative movement. It is the anti-matter, which destroys matter, it is the black hole, where no light escapes it, it is the void, which creates the big bang. It is the orgasm of all orgasms; it is where non-linear reality folds onto itself to create a sphere, and it is the place where myths are being birthed. What you call your reality is a form of a temporary illusion accepted by most outside the delusional, the mentally ill, the schizoid, and the crazy. In essence you came here and over time formed a false reality that is now in the process of deconstruction, and implosion. Common sense, science, and logic are all on the defense, and myth, superstition, angst, rumors, and unstable emotional waves are covering over many who are not strong enough to decipher truth from false.

It is a moment in time where anything seems possible because the rules of the game are changing, and the new rules are yet to be fully formed. Many realize that if they can't trust logic and science then anything can replace them. Even spirit is not exempt from waves of deconstruction. New incomplete spiritual systems are being introduced as truths, spiritual misinformation is abundant, half-baked techniques are being invented daily and introduced as wholesome only adding to the confusion of the bursting bubble.

In the midst of all this there is your heart, there is your light, there is your truth, there is your love. These are all states of being not of doing. Connecting requires you to slow down, be in silence, stop acting, and connect to your feelings without reacting, aligning the emotional, with the mental and the physical creating a coherent ripple, one that is so powerful that it neutralizes all the noise, the confusion, the fear that is around you.

Some of you indeed came here to do things, but more as a secondary mission. The primary mission of many old souls was to hold the planetary fulcrum in balance; your job is to "be," and as you walk in your "beingness" you affect all and all is affected by you.

We will be supporting your wings when you are tired from being who you came here to be but we cannot "be" for you.

Before we close the gap and move beyond the veil, we wish to remind you to not let the urge to love everyone and do good distract you from your main mission, which is self-love. Self-love is the gate to true service, only through self-love can you ever truly love another. Your gift is limited by your capacity to love self. When you have forgiven the self and accepted it fully, you are ready to facilitate shift that ripples to all that cross your path.

Wake up to your power, your commitment, and your truth, and remove distractions, remove strategies, and take time to feel more deeply than you ever had.

When you go to sleep at night ask to remember, when you wake up in the morning ask to remember, and when you are in confusion ask to remember. It is all within you, and it is time to remember why you came here. You are so dearly loved, and so be it.

Conflict

We missed you, like you have missed us. We are never too far apart. You are a part of us and we are a part of you. Like a child in the womb of her mother. Although they do not communicate verbally, they are one. We and you are one. You summon us when you are sad, when you are in conflict, when drama rattles you, but know that we are with you always, in joy and in despair, for good and for bad and even death does not do us apart.

You have questions, many questions. You believe that we can answer them, but we cannot. It is not a part of our job descriptions. If anything, our job is more aligned with asking you even more questions. The questions propel you forward. The answer satisfies your appetite for closure.

You exist in a holographic reality in which all that you have ever been in the past is connected to your now and to what you call future. In actuality, there is no past, there is no future, there is only ever present and when you are fully in the present all questions dissipate. They are not necessary, they do not serve, and there is only one answer to all of them: *Be present to what is.* When you are inhaling and exhaling, being fully in the present, your answer is, *I am.* This is the only possible answer to the question.

We hear you protest, *But I want to know!* We say to you, *But you do know.*

Where should I turn left or right, you ask?

Our answer is always the same: *It does not matter.*

How would I improve on the life that I have chosen to live? you ask. And we say, *Be present.*

How would I accomplish more? Live up to my full potential? Make more money? Be loving to my friends? Leave a legacy? Be of service?

It is our turn to ask you, *Why do you believe that this is what you came here to do and be? What is being good? Why accomplish more? And what is service?*

You are in service being alive. Your very existence is your service. Coming here is your accomplishment, your reason to come here is not "to do" but "to be." What you "do" should "be" an extension of that and not the other way around. About being good!? That is a concept that you have been spoon-fed since birth. Good is relative, being "good" to one, may be "bad" for another. There is no such thing as absolute good, there is only truth, your truth. Truth is relative, but your truth is absolute. When you are in a relationship and you are faced with an oxymoron, being accommodating to your partner is being "good," but serving yourself is "bad." You may miss the purpose for your being. All aspects of you, including your partner, children, extended family, friends, work, and outer reality, conspire to do one thing, serve you to become who you are, to live your truth, to be free. They appear in your life because your entity summons them to teach you about you. When you make your life mission to accommodate others, you do not progress, as there is no learning. You are a reality magician, all of you. All that you perceive around you is your own creation; you have invited all the actors and circumstances in your life to teach you about you. Your learning is to be present, to absorb the lesson; imbibe it and reflect it back through physical expression. Your sole purpose is to be you. Your unique melody is the service that you came here to share. You do not come here to be relative, you come here to be absolute, you do not come here to accommodate, you come here to express your uniqueness.

The conflicts that appear in your life are your interpretation of situations that put you at odds with you. All conflicts are inner movements. When you are aligned with you, there can never be a conflict. When you are fully in the present there can never be a conflict. Conflict is defined in your language as a collision, a contradiction, an opposition, all which imply an agenda that is not being fulfilled. What if you came without an agenda, what if all your options were equally satisfying and all you needed to express was the one aligned with your truth? Would there be grounds for a conflict? Your surrounding may tag it as a conflict but for you it won't be. It will only be a movement, an expression, an extension of who you are.

The conflict begins with wanting, wishing, aspiring, having an ambition, a yearning, an expectation. You grow to believe that these things are necessary, but we invite you to consider that all the strife and discontent in your reality here on this planet originate from that which you are taught to believe early on.

Then why does a baby cry out when it does not get food or human warmth, for example? Surely it has not yet been influenced by its environment? A baby acts from its physical needs which are built into its form. It knows what it needs, and it is clear. Let's call it a she. A baby girl has a pure distinction between needs and wanting. She does not cry because she did not get a dress she liked, or the newest smart phone. She cries because her basic needs are not met, and she is letting the world know. She is in her complete truth. There are no filters placed on her voice, her agenda, her desires. She demands that her needs be met with the knowledge that it is natural that these needs would be met.

What you are asked to consider is that you call the shots, even as young as a baby. You create what you need by expressing your needs. When later on, your needs take on a whole different spectrum, they are no longer just basic needs. They are self-created needs that result in conflict. A baby does not have a conflict. It knows what it needs, and she is asking for it. As an adult, you do not know what you need because your needs, as well as everyone else's needs, get thrown together into a confusing soup, to a point where you lose sight and distinctions between your needs and others. You become an extension of something other than you. Your own needs become muddled. It is on you to filter what is yours and demand it like the baby. When you do, the universe, like your mother, will satisfy your needs.

But we have heard of cases where the mother does not fulfill her baby's needs, yes indeed, and that is a choice of a spirit to experience a difficult and challenging environment early on. The soul is ageless, and it seeks what it needs to grow. Such circumstances are known before birth, selected in advance, and often relate to karmic agreements.

Understand that it is a school here on your precious planet. It is a school that teaches you about you, about choice, about love, and about reality creation.

It is a school that grades you not on your achievements, accomplishments, the wealth you create, and how loved you are, but primarily for showing up, and then for how accurate you played yourself. You are not getting trophies when you play yourself, but you progress, and you grow, which is the purpose of your coming here.

Sit with us for just a moment, breathe deeply, relax into your body, feel your heart beat. Know that you are a timeless, ageless, eternal being, going through a journey that never really ends. You have all the time as there is no time, you have all the space because there is infinite space, and most importantly, you are loved throughout without judgment, so do settle into your own heart, and know that whether you choose left or right, you are loved just the same.

Remember the pure baby that just emerged, and ask in your heart what you need, and discard needs that are not yours; be fully present at each and every moment with your eyes open, gazing directly at what is in front of you. What is in front of you is the only thing you must consider in your now.

How can we plan for our future, our children's future? We ask you to consider that the future is made out of the now, so focus on being truthful; you will teach your children to do the same, by example. Your plans often get swiped by what you consider your reality. Instead of focusing on what will be, focus on your heartbeat. All time stems from that moment, even what you consider your future.

That is very scary, not to worry about the future. Indeed, that is an angelic joke. It is "scary" not to "worry." You use fear and use worrying to feel better. Why not discard the fear and the worrying and just feel better being here now in the moment?

Humans are an enigma; angels are human in training. We offer you to go back to be a baby, see what your real needs are, and scream them at the top of your lungs. We promise you that Mother Earth and your reality will fulfill these needs as they come from the pure version of you.

We are you and you are us; together we make the great "I am." We are grateful to come to you today and at any other time that you summon us. We love you and are with you every step of the way, and so be it.

Birth

What does the birth of a human signify? you ask. You celebrate the day you enter into this realm, but to us it is almost the opposite. From being "all-knowing" you agree to move into a realm where a great deal is initially hidden from you, until it is revealed.

For us, birth is a celebration in one dimension, but it is also a loss in another. Your energy never dies, nor do you lose consciousness of who you are. Even when you lie unconscious, or as you call it, in a vegetative state, your energy is still awake and alert. There are no circumstances that threaten your existence. Your birth is simply moving away from one reality to another for a short while. Then you return. It is that simple.

When you are born to what you call physical life, it is a celebration because you passed the entry exams and entered into a challenging period of learning. It is also a loss because at the time that you are in a physical body, your other expanded aspect or self is on hold and in a non-responsive state. You stop communicating with your friends (in the other dimension) and going on excursions like you would normally.

On the one side, you are in a state of pause, and on the other, you are in an active state. Very few in your past have been able to hold both states alert and awake. When you are in a physical body, it takes an immense amount of energy to contain the vastness of your being. Some of you have very limited access to this other dimension. We discussed in various messages the process of selecting your circumstances, your parents, future appointments, husbands, wives, lovers, children, enemies, adversaries, challenges, paths, etc.

After your physical birth, you forget all your prior preparations and just live your life. When you "die" it also signifies your birth to the other dimension. The same celebration takes place on the other side except that you remember both your earthly life and remain fully aware of your current angelic life.

We call the other life "angelic" not because something changes that turns you into an angel. What has changed is your awareness and comprehension of who you *really* are. Why is it so difficult to hold onto the angelic frequency in the physical dimension after birth? some might ask. The answer has to do with gravity. Your body is dense, your movements slow (in comparison).... In a physical form, you need to eat and drink. With a body, you experience "lack" including hunger, thirst, pain, fear, and depression. You also are able to experience joy, pleasure, love, happiness, and excitement. Because you are in a dense reality, you do not know the entirety of who you are. Thus you do not trust that you are looked after, that all of your challenges are designed by you. Due to the influence of gravitational forces, the more dense you become, the less your body can hold onto the subtle yet expansive frequency of your angelic reality. The denser you are, the less access you have. The lighter you are, the less weight you carry, the greater your access to our realm. As a result, the subtler realm gates are more readily available to you. The clearer your field, the more you are able to contain and be in tune with the subtler realm, allowing you to read its signs and follow its guidance.

You may ask, How do we become lighter? We have tried all the diets out there and none seem to work. It is not your waist-line that we speak of, but the quality of your thoughts, all of which are influenced by what you eat, drink, consume, watch, breath, do, and don't do. Your physical actions on the gravity plane significantly determine your weight. For example, air carries oxygen. The deeper your breath, the more oxygen enters your blood stream, which greatly enhances your body's functions and ability to relax or respond to stress. Breathing air is the one action that you must perform all the time in order to stay alive. The more you master this action, the lighter you become. Most of you tend to have shallow breathing; you may even taint your breathing by smoking or because you live in a very polluted area.

The quality and substance of your breath is essential to your ability to connect to the path an animal such as a cow, sheep, goat, chicken, or fish has to go through before being slaughtered en route to your dinner plate. That path dictates your weight. If the process of their slaughter was committed humanely as a sacred event, done by honoring with sensitivity, compassion, and gratitude, that is what you will ingest. If the process was inhumane, fear-ridden, and brutally painful, that is also what you will ingest. If the animal consumed poison before it reached your plate, that is what you will digest. What you eat is who you are. When you digest a living being that was killed to fill your hunger, you take its fear, which often translates to the production of hormones like adrenalin, which flood the body of the animal within nano-seconds. When you ingest that living being, your body breaks down and takes in everything. How many people have kidney issues because of overly active adrenal glands? Fear-based panic and anxiety attacks as well as depression are partially a result of the residues of the food you digest, a "gift" from the animals you slaughtered.

Do you truly believe that you must eat a living being to survive? The more connected to spirit a society is, the less livestock they consume. You are spirit, and so are the other live beings you eat. The more slaughter is done on your behalf, the more fear and pain you ingest through the live beings you consume, the heavier a vibration you carry, which in turn decreases your access to the subtler realms. In your cultures, the Yogi, Brahmin, and Holy men and women all tend to consume a vegetarian diet. They do so *not* because they don't enjoy the taste, but because the gates to the subtler realms require a higher vibration. In the Abrahamic traditions, the spiritual realm is more violent and heavy in content, context, and dogma, partially because of the diet. The more peaceful a culture's tradition, the less live beings it consumes. There is never a judgment on our side as to what you consume. All your choices are equally honored, however the purpose of our message is to shine light on the different aspects of your journey so that you may choose what best suits you.

You might ask, why should we make an effort to remain connected to our subtler realm? After all, we have important things to worry about such as our health, finances, safety, and survival.

We find it funny that you insist on worrying. There are many advantages to remaining connected to the subtler realms. The subtler realms allow you to know when your health is imbalanced while guiding you on how to correct the imbalance. The subtler realms allow you to remain connected to the natural abundance to which you are entitled, without ever having to experience scarcity. The subtler realms will guide you before you enter into a dangerous situation, so that you may avoid threats altogether. By removing the fear for survival (because you are connected to your subtler form), you live your life knowing that you are an eternal being. If you insist on calling a doctor when you don't feel well, or decide to chase wealth, accumulate incestuously and excessively, carry guns, hire guards, pay for an army to protect you, build walls and shelters, accumulate food reserves, inhabit Mars, or pilfer from others in order to survive, then these are your choices. Everything is honored, but then again, why would you do such things if you didn't have to?

After breathing and eating come your thoughts. Your thoughts create your reality, which are in turn affected by your breathing and consumption. You experience your reality through your senses, which is interpreted by your mind. Your head is always switched "on." The quality of your thoughts determines how you view the world.... Is it a friendly and hospitable, benevolent place, or violent and dangerous? Learning to control your thoughts—instead of your thoughts controlling you—changes the way you perceive the world. Quieting an overly-active mind lightens your load and expands your idea of who you are, and what your role is here on this physical plane. Your mind will object, as it doesn't want to be on furlough. Your mind wants to be active because when it is, it becomes aware of its own importance and existence.

The fourth angle of the pyramid that supports the quality of your vibration is your sexual center. It must be clear of shame and guilt, activated and alive. Your ability to be light vibrating and connected to your extended family, combined with your capacity to hold more of the field of your greater "I am," is intimately linked to your sexuality. Not how much sex you are having, but the quality, vibrancy, clarity, and power of this center. Your sexuality holds your power; it is your engine. The more you work to keep it clean and to distill its fuel, the higher the octane and the more power you have to access. Shame and guilt are the largest contributors to clogging this center, followed by abuse, a poor self-image, a lack of self-love, and the inability to derive pleasure from self and others through sacred sexuality.

The quality of your breath, the consumption of food and liquids, the quality of your thoughts, and the quality of your sexual energy are the main components of the four-sided pyramid. The apex is yourself, love, and the I AM. It's all about the way you treat yourself. All other vertices of the pyramid support Self-love.

If you were to duplicate the pyramid underneath itself, upside down, it would become an octahedron.

By observing the lines beneath the surface, you would be able to see the negative culprit responsible for holding you in a heavier place, a gravity-based reality.

The quality and pollution of your breathing resources, the pollution and excessive use of food resources, the competition of your attention via the constant bombardment of stimulants, and the tainting of your sexual powers through institutions (such as the law, popular culture, parental guidance, and your own self-created guilt and shame) result in self-hatred and self-loathing.

At any point, you have a choice. You have come here to experience the buffet and to choose the journey that fits you. We have told you that you come here to awaken. Only those who have in them that seed will have access to this message, so if and when you read it, know that this is why you are here—to awaken—and for you to awaken, you must form a relationship with your spirit. To be able to listen to your spirit, you must become subtle and lighten up your load. We shine light on your journey, but we will not walk it for you. We are you and you are us, and when we merge we are the Great I AM. Awaken and walk. Sacred this walk is, and you chose to be here now because you have a role to play. Play it and so be it.

Message Guide

A Tree — "Be the tree, we say to you, and do not go on worrying about the well-being of the forest before you've mastered being the tree. Your most powerful contribution to the forest that you are part of is being the most magnificent tree." (p. 5)

The Threshold — "There are doorways that were meant for you to walk through, and in each lifetime, you may pass by many of them and never open a single one. And then comes a cycle—and sacred this cycle is—when you become aware of the doors, and one by one you open them and walk through. Each door opened creates a pulse that changes the universal beat around you. Each door opened introduces a new frequency to your reality, and each new reality allows you to soar higher. This is your time and your mission, to open these doors and walk through." (p. 10)

Knock, Knock — "A knock can take the form of an accident, an illness, loss of a relative or loved one, a traumatic separation from your lover or child, a divorce, loss of job or income, loss of a home to fire, flood, or foreclosure, depression, or physical ailments that restrict your movements. Each knock is asking you to open a door inside of you." (p. 16)

Being Alive — "You are asked to let go of your old safety nets, and trust that you will be guided. Being in service to Self and Earth means that you are no longer guided by desires to go somewhere and be attached to outcomes. You allow that which presents itself to you and offer gratitude in an exchange. You move about as if you are using your wings more than your feet. Trust that whatever serves you will appear in your physical dimension to support your path, and whatever is hampering your path must be discarded, making space for the new." (p. 23)

The Difference Between A Human and An Angel — "A human, who turns angel, plants seeds of light everywhere she sets foot. As she walks, people's hearts open, hands that were clutched surrender, and eyes that were shut closed begin to sparkle. The vibration emanating from a meeting between the one who embodies love and the one who opens her heart to love is like a reunion of twin souls. They merge, and both are changed forever. Love expands and light illuminates. Your role is to be a bridge, a conduit, a lover, and to allow that which crosses your path to touch your heart, without having your heart change colors. You are a vibration, a melody, a frequency, which manifests in form." (p. 29–30)

Nothing and Everything — "Let go of who you think you should become, let go of your idea of limitation, let go of your inadequacies, let go of your ideas of good and bad, let go of separation. Let go of anything onto which you previously held. Let go of fears, let go of wanting, let go of any idea about who you are or what you are." (p. 35)

The Sphinx — "Your ancestors knew that there is no rush to get anywhere. They held sacred that all movements are but an expression of a flow back and forth within a sphere. All that goes up must come down and all that sways to the left must also sway to the right. Their main ambition was to be aligned with the universal flow that was manifested all around their physical reality. Unlike you, they wanted to read the map and walk in alignment with the charted path. You are, at the moment, out of balance with the universal flow, as you have veered from the path of reading the map, and you are attempting to force your will on the universal laws around you." (p. 38–9)

Limbo — "For every time that you feel darkness, know that you are making space for light. Each time you take a leap not knowing if you'll end up at the bottom of a pit never to be found again, or lying on a bed of roses, know that you have moved in alignment with your role. You must move, change, create, explore, open, and open some more. Then, when you feel that you can no longer open because you will fall apart and become discombobulated, you are asked to trust and open some more." (p. 47)

Lost Innocence — "It is time, now, to link with the purity of the child you once were. It is essential to connect with the pure heart of carefree laughter. It is sacred to look again at your body like an infant discovering her toes for the first time. When you were little, all aspects of your body were equally sacred and you were just beginning to learn what is yours and what is not. You had yet to place a judgment on good, bad, appropriate, or inappropriate. We ask you to find that space in you again." (p. 51)

The Test — "Your love of self is being tested and your core truth is being pushed to its limits. Hold on to nothing and move with the wind. Do not resist the pain, and do not resist the agony. Move deeper into yourself and you will find that in the deepest cavern of your heart there is only light and it shines so bright that it forgives and holds compassion for each human regardless of their choices." (p. 56)

The Rainbow — "Being free is embracing the totality of existence within the spectrum of the rainbow, creating a circle that is a reflection of light, where each hue represents the angle of the light hitting the raindrops. None of it is 'you' and all of it is 'you.' It is time for you to be free from holding on to how others perceive you. Clear your attachments, sever the cords, break the chains, and move away from the human angel's ambivalent duality-based consciousness, acknowledging that once you have crossed the threshold, there is no going back." (p. 61)

Two Become One — "There is always a purpose of two coming together, the timing of a beginning and the timing of an ending are as sacred as any birth and death. When two become one they, in fact, become three. Long before you have created a child through birth you have created a third being that is the two forms merged. You come into unions as a creative act, and each time you merge you have created a new form." (p. 68)

The Cell — "The cell is conscious in the same way that the human is conscious. Indeed there are levels of awareness, but each cell has an awareness of self and its environment. The macro and the micro are always linked, reflecting the same basic truth." (p. 73)

The Divine Plan — "If you knew truly and completely that you are loved, cared for, protected, and guided, would you still have a reason to worry, be scared, be a victim? If you knew that you can never fail on this journey, and that all lessons end up serving the divine plan, regardless of whether its intent came from dark or light, would you still doubt that you are where you need to be?" (p. 79)

Layers — "... [L]ayers are like shadows of the past. They appear, then disappear as quickly, once you have illuminated their essence by using love. As soon as one shadow is illuminated, a new shadow appears, all different, yet the same. All come from movies left unfinished. All movement seeks to find equilibrium before clearing away. Most of you are now in the midst of opening your dusty moldy attics, clearing away unfinished stories, some of which are very old. This is why you are now easily overwhelmed, as debris of all types, shapes, and sizes comes at you, seemingly from arbitrary directions. You are here in the now, clearing the past so you can move into a new future." (p. 87)

Into the Fire — "The journey of an angel dressed up as a human is to go into the fire and emerge intact. The only power that can motivate you to walk into the fire is love. The only power that can lead you safely and intact out of the fire is love. Your soul family is your main tool to teach you about love from all angles. It is a framework for learning. If you were not in school would you spend much of your waking hours completing your homework? Your soul family is your school and it presents you with an incentive to do your homework." (p. 94)

Reboot — "When a car swerves off its course, hitting you, and you get injured, your external aspect and internal aspect have just collided. The result of the collision, besides the obvious pain and medical treatment that you must undergo, is that your external and internal vibrational field align for a moment. You may call it rebooting." (p. 99)

Gratitude — "The power of true gratitude is in its shape. It is shaped like a tetrahedron key. This key opens the gate to true knowing, to true surrender, and to a true acceptance of this union. Spirit wishes to express itself; the ego within the physical vehicle wishes to express itself; the body wishes to express itself. All expressions are in balance only when the entire being is in gratitude." (p. 104)

The Player — "You cannot hide your thoughts, feelings, and actions from the 'I am.' It is all-knowing, and regardless of what everyone thinks about you, your God-self knows, and it will ask you to account for your choices, to face your lower self. You can be the most sophisticated player, who can hide your true self from everyone, playing the game of light to perfection, but you cannot hide from your 'I am.' Your higher aspect, the one who guides you along the trajectory, higher and higher, knows who you are, and, with love, and through love, will have you face yourself. There is no escaping the speeding traffic police because the judge, jury, and plaintiff are all within you." (p. 112–3)

The Game of Your Life — "This is why you came here. You take your life so seriously that we must give you a little reminder of why you are here and the larger scope of your playing field. You come here to play, and before you enter this playing field, you set up for yourself the ground rules, you plan moves, and you strategize so you can play a 'good' game. But often, as you play the game, you forget that it is just a game and you lose sight of why you came here to begin with." (p. 117)

The Endgame — "*What is the endgame?* you wish to know.

You stop playing their game, is our answer. As long as you play it, you cannot neutralize it or change it. The endgame cannot be determined by a tug of war with powers, each pulling on opposite sides. This form of reality-making is messy, dualistic at its core, and does not recognize the divinity and choice each has, to birth their own vision. Systems are based upon groups, which agree to certain rules. No system can survive without willing participants, not even for a day." (p. 124)

What If — "(What) If you were told that your world was coming to an end, would you do anything different? Would you hug more? Forgive more? Love more? Relax more? If you were told that, at the end of this day, you are going to be finished here, would you live the seconds, moments, or hours you have left differently than you would have if that information was not available?" (p. 129)

The Gate — "When you walk through a gate, it always involves resistance, so expect it, honor it, and celebrate. Walking through gates requires conquering fear, very real, existential fear, fear of death. Expect it, celebrate it, honor it, and congratulate yourself while walking with eyes open. If it did not involve fear it would not be a gate. Walking from one field of vibration to another requires courage, trust, surrender, perseverance, persistence, humility, and authenticity." (p. 133)

Darkness — "What if we told you that, in this reality, it is precisely the thing you hate, the thing you complain about so much, that is also the precise reason you are here? To live through it, to know it, to make peace with it, to learn to transmute it, to transform it, and to know that darkness and light are states of being, intimately connected. You came here to expand your idea of the shadow, to look at the range of grays and to review any idea you had about the spectrum, maybe even to suspend judgment about the dark, and to suspend judgment about the light." (p. 137)

Happiness — "Those who are indeed happy are those who do not seek happiness; those who bathe in joy are those who do not go out trying to be joyful; and those who are in bliss are those who gave up on searching and are firmly anchored in just being." (p. 142)

The Trench — "The trench is your default path, the one that is set up for you, if you chose to keep on sleeping in a particular lifetime. Once awakened, the first call of the day is to climb up the slippery, tall walls of the trench and get out. This is the way it always works. There is little movement when you are asleep. There is a celebration on our side as you begin to awaken." (p. 150–1)

Fulcrum — "Some of you indeed came here to do things, but more as a secondary mission. The primary mission of many old souls was to hold the planetary fulcrum in balance; your job is to 'be,' and as you walk in your 'beingness' you affect all and all is affected by you." (p. 154)

Conflict — "Conflict is defined in your language as a collision, a contradiction, an opposition, all which imply an agenda that is not being fulfilled. What if you came without an agenda, what if all your options were equally satisfying and all you needed to express was the one aligned with your truth? Would there be grounds for a conflict? Your surrounding may tag it as a conflict but for you it won't be. It will only be a movement, an expression, an extension of who you are." (p. 156–7)

Birth — "For us, birth is a celebration in one dimension, but it is also a loss in another. Your energy never dies, nor do you lose consciousness of who you are. Even when you lie unconscious, or as you call it, in a vegetative state, your energy is still awake and alert. There are no circumstances that threaten your existence. Your birth is simply moving away from one reality to another for a short while. Then you return. It is that simple." (p. 160)

Acknowledgments

I dedicate this book to my Father, Igal Ashuah, who passed away 2-26-2018.

I offer my utmost gratitude and love to all of the human angels who held and supported me through some very difficult times in my life. Thanks to my dear and loving friends: you have made this journey possible with your heart and so much more colorful and exciting. You know who you are, and I am forever indebted for your love in my life.

Special thanks to Corinne Gervai for your invaluable input and support and to Gisela Stromeyer for your encouragement and unwavering belief in this work. I am forever grateful to you.

I wish to thank my publisher, Paul Cohen, designer Colin Rolfe and the team at Epigraph Publishing for their unwavering support. I also wish to thank my editor Gabrielle Euvino for helping me and guiding me with great care.

At the end, I wish to thank my teachers' guides, both those who came before me, as well as those who will come after me. I wish to offer my gratitude to all of those who hold the light and shine, especially in the face of adversity and darkness. I wish to offer my heartfelt gratitude to the world of the unseen angels... you never cease to astonish and teach me about the vast spectrum of hues that surrounds a human.

At the end of this game of life, there is only Love.

With Gratitude and Love,
Dror

www.conversationwithangels.com

Dror Ashuah is an internationally recognized inspirational speaker, intuitive, and channel. He is author of the book series *Conversation with Angels* (Epigraph/Monkfish Book Publishing Company), a collection of messages on spiritual awakening received by Dror from the Angelic (or spiritual) realm in preparation for this unprecedented time of global change.

Mr. Ashuah earned a Master's degree from Harvard University in Human Development and Psychology. His extensive worldwide travels combined with studies in mysticism, astrology, Reiki, crystals, and Shamanism have all contributed to his personal understanding of the messages about human consciousness.

Dror's powerful and inspirational workshops reach his audience in a deep and transformational manner. Dror relays a non-linear worldview about the nature of life on Earth and our greater purpose in the Universe: awakening to our divinity and understanding our spiritual role on this earthly journey.

Printed in Poland
by Amazon Fulfillment
Poland Sp. z o.o., Wrocław

13895435R00117